Overview of the Sociolinguistic Context of the Dongxiang Language

ŁÓDŹ STUDIES IN LANGUAGE

Edited by Barbara Lewandowska-Tomaszczyk and Łukasz Bogucki

VOLUME 77

Julie P. M. Lefort

Overview of the Sociolinguistic Context of the Dongxiang Language

PETER LANG
Berlin · Bruxelles · Chennai · Lausanne · New York · Oxford

Bibliographic Information published by the Deutsche Nationalbibliothek
The Deutsche Nationalbibliothek lists this publication in the Deutsche Nationalbibliografie; detailed bibliographic data is available online at http://dnb.d-nb.de.

Library of Congress Cataloging-in-Publication Data
A CIP catalog record for this book has been applied for at the Library of Congress.
LCCN 2025012545

The cover image courtesy of Benjamin Ben Chaim.

The publication was funded by the Agence nationale de la recherche (ANR, French National Agency for Research) funded project 'Language contact in Northern China – Historical and Typological perspectives' (LCNC, Programme CE27, ANR 2018) and coordinated by Prof. Redouane Djamouri (CNRS, CRLAO, Paris).
ISSN 1437-5281
ISBN 978-3-631-92181-4 (Print)
ISBN 978-3-631-93911-6 (E-PDF)
ISBN 978-3-631-93912-3 (E-PUB)
DOI 10.3726/b22983

Published by Peter Lang GmbH, Berlin (Germany)

info@peterlang.com

This publication has been peer reviewed.

www.peterlang.com

Abstract

This study aims at questioning the relationship of language and identity through the description of the sociolinguistic environment of the Dongxiang language, an under-studied Mongolic language spoken by the Dongxiang people in Southern Gansu, China. Through a sociolinguistic analysis, we will try to understand how, through interaction between the Dongxiang people and their neighbouring Hui communities, and their relationship to Standard Chinese, language contacts have deeply modified the structure of the Dongxiang language. The Dongxiang linguistic community is in a state of unconscious diglossia: there is *de facto* a hierarchy of languages, but it is not recognised by speakers and is not expressed in the form of a general feeling of linguistic insecurity within the community. This is reflected in the Dongxiang language, where a specific morphology has been developed to integrate lexical and syntactic borrowings, making code-switching and code-mixing virtually impossible.

Keywords: Dongxiang language; Linxia dialect; Diglossia; Contact-induced change; Code-switching; Linguistic community dynamics

Dedication

I dedicate this study to all the Dongxiang people. Special thanks are due to Fatima, who welcomed me into her home with open arms, along with Ma Yanhong and Axiye, who were my consultants for the duration of this study and who became my friends.

Table of Contents

Figures, Maps and Photos

Tables

Preface

In 2009, when I first visited the Dongxiang Autonomous County to conduct fieldwork, I was struck by how 'backward' the whole area was in terms of economics and infrastructure development as compared to the rest of China. The eastern part of the country, in particular – where I had already spent a few years – had started to blossom 10 years before. Dongxiang had poor road connections, even to the district 'capital' Suonanba (锁南坝), and some villages were not even accessible by car. Although electricity was widely available, some villages were still not connected to the main water supply and had to rely on wells. At the time, the level of poverty was the highest in China, as was the level of illiteracy in Chinese. During my fieldwork, I met almost 200 people. Among these, most women from my generation could only read one or two characters, while men who had received more than 3 years of education at primary school were rare. Most professional activities focused on agriculture, and cultural life centred around the mosques and religious life. In the main town of Suonanba, trade was limited to the weekly market for food and basic necessities, along with the cattle and the coal markets. There was a main street with about 50 shops, including a 'modern accommodation' (and a small supermarket attached to it), which was the *Mínzú dàshà* (民族大厦), the County's 'minority hotel', where officials from outside stayed when visiting. The other commercial areas were in Narisi (娜日斯) and Daban (达板), two other towns (*zhèn* 镇) in the county. And there was not much else in Dongxiang – only small stores were to be found in some villages. Outside the towns, most household's staple food such as dairy products and bread were produced at home on a daily basis, not only because it was an economical way to access them, but also because there was no place to buy them. Although parts of the county were partially connected to the surrounding regions and more developed than others, Dongxiang was isolated and left behind the 'high-speed economic train' that the rest of China was on. It was almost as if time had stopped in the late 1980s, when the Chinese government had last initiated the construction of the few buildings that could still be seen in the various local administrative towns (*zhèn* 镇) scattered across the region. Another remarkable phenomenon was the scarcity of men present in the countryside villages. As opposed to the rest of China, where both parents worked as migrant labourers in the cities and children were left in the care of their grandparents in the countryside, the women of Dongxiang remained with their elders and children, and were responsible for farming activities while the men worked in the cities. Because of this specific context, and although bilingualism with the Chinese variety of Linxia was already widespread at the time, the Dongxiang language was not endangered. The developmental backwardness of the whole area – in terms of education, economic development, and communication – as well as the fact that Dongxiang was vividly spoken in rural areas and transmitted to children through women were the reasons why, at the time, no one believed that the Dongxiang language would disappear in the near future. Neither could the drastic sociological and socio-economical changes that were to take place over the next 15 years be foreseen.

This book is based on data collected in this specific environment in 2009 and 2010 for my PhD thesis, which I defended in 2012. It was later updated using existing literature and additional data available up until 2016. One might wonder: why is it important to publish this study 15 years after the data were collected?

First, since the data were collected, the fieldwork as it was carried out at the time could not be conducted again in the same manner. The main reason being that, in 2011, the Chinese government passed the "People's Republic of China intangible cultural heritage Law" (*Zhōnghuá Rénmín Gònghéguó fēi wùzhí wénhuà yíchǎn fǎ* 中华人民共和国非物质文化遗产法), requiring foreign researchers to be supervised and supported by local government officials in collaboration with academic peers[1]. The notion 'Intangible cultural heritage' includes languages, linguistic and sociolinguistic data; therefore, the field is no longer freely accessible, the collectable data and the methods of data collection are subject to prior approval of the local authorities[2]. Access to information in Dongxiang was already difficult in 2009–2010, but mainly for social reasons: the Dongxiang community was still very isolated, and people coming to their villages to conduct surveys was restricted to government officials. Accordingly, although the number of informants in this study may seem small compared to other sociolinguistic studies conducted in other parts of the world – or even within China – it is still substantial because of this particular context. Another aspect to take into consideration is that it would not have been possible to repeat such a large-scale interview in Dongxiang after this study, for other political reasons that I will further explain below. To date, this is the only study of its kind on language representation and diglossia, in Chinese and in a Western language. Indeed, research exploring sociolinguistic data in Dongxiang is otherwise limited to case-studies specific to particular villages, mostly conducted by Chinese scholars. Second, although partial economic and demographic data are available to the public and researchers, surveys are limited in number, and the nature of the data collected in terms of language and ethnicity has been restricted by the Chinese government. It would therefore be difficult to obtain the same kind of data that was collected at the time, and update it to reflect the current context. Third, and most importantly, the economic and urban development driven by national and local policies has led to the restructuration of the Dongxiang Autonomous County, transforming its demography and social organisation. This shift has had a direct impact on the vitality of the Dongxiang language, and its interaction with the surrounding local Chinese dialects. The first step was the development of roads

1 Cf article 15 « 境外组织在中华人民共和国境内进行非物质文化遗产调查，应当与境内非物质文化遗产学术研究机构合作进行 » ['Foreign organisations conducting surveys on intangible cultural heritage in the People's Republic of China shall do so in collaboration with domestic academic research institutions for intangible cultural heritage']. <https://www.gov.cn/flfg/2011-02/25/content_1857449.htm> (consulted on 20/11/2024).

2 Cf article 15 of the People's Republic of China intangible cultural inheritage Law.

and infrastructure to connect all villages and make them accessible by car. From 2012 to 2014, the Dongxiang Autonomous district was chosen as 'a pilot county for poverty alleviation through transport'[3]. A number of large-scale projects were initiated not only to connect all the villages of Dongxiang by road, but also to better connect the County itself to the existing surrounding networks. Among other projects, the National highway 213 was built, connecting Lanzhou to Linxia via Dongxiang, along with 120 rural roads, covering a total of 1,209 km[4]. This had a significant impact on road transport, especially in the most remote areas, where, prior to such changes, children often had to walk for several hours to reach schools. It also increased people's mobility and goods transportation, leading to fast economic development and access to a whole new range of products for the Dongxiang people. As roads improved, more children were able to access education, and the literacy level in Chinese slightly increased. Furthermore, this period saw the development of Suonanba as an 'economic hub' that completely reshaped the environment of the township. The main changes were architectural and related to space organisation: a 'communist style' central square, brand new administrative buildings, a cultural area with a museum and a park including artworks related to the Dongxiang culture (partly creating a new artificially 'branded' identity for them at the same time), and commercial areas that could house restaurants, shops and entertainment areas were built within the course of 2 years. At last, and more recently, the 'Poverty Alleviation through Relocation project' (PAR – *yìdì fúpín bānqiān zhèngcè* 易地扶贫搬迁政策), launched in 2016, which aims to 'win the battle against extreme poverty' (*dǎyíng tuōpín gōngjiānzhàn* 打赢脱贫攻坚战), has resulted in the relocation of poor people from inhospitable areas. As part of this policy, China planned to build 35,000 settlement communities (*xīn kāifāqū* 新开发区 'newly developed areas') by 2023 and relocate 9.6 million people from rural areas to newly built modern townships[5]. In 2018, Dongxiang had relocated 9,793 people, and 28,023 people in 2020. There is no more precise data after that date. I personally visited three of the 'newly developed towns' in Suonanba, Narisi and Daban. It is clear

---

3 省上将我县列为全省扶贫攻坚交通先行试点县等重大政策机遇。

4 <https://www.dxzzzx.gov.cn/dxx/zwdt/dxyw/art/2022/art_58eeef7b76eb479488306ac7f4130ba5.html> (consulted on 15/11/2024).

5 See references in Liu et al. (2023).

that these phenomena are profoundly reshaping the linguistic environment of the Dongxiang speakers, affecting their traditional ways of living and communicating, as well as the relationships between men and women, and the relationship between children and their mother tongue.

Another aspect of the changes I have witnessed in the sociolinguistic landscape of Dongxiang (which is, in fact, visible throughout China) is directly related to the various policies concerning minorities and their languages, but also to the efforts made by the Chinese government to strengthen the national language, through policies that do not overtly target such minorities. Over the past decade, these policies have prioritised the strengthening of the national language over linguistic diversity, which includes minority languages as well as Chinese dialects (Grey, forthcoming 2025). Unlike some other minorities in the region, such as Tibetans and Mongolians, the Dongxiang people has never had a largely spread out written tradition for their language[6], and the Dongxiang language has never been taught in schools as a subject. However, the Dongxiang language has been used as a medium of instruction, and the impact of these policies has been the same as for any other Chinese national minority. In 2021, during his important speech (*zhòngyàojiǎnghuà* 重要讲话) delivered at the Central Ethnic Work Conference (*Zhōngyāng mínzú gōngzuòhuìyì* 中央民族工作会议),[7] Xi Jiping announced that the main objective of these policies was to 'strengthen the sense of community among the Chinese people'[8] through the promotion of unity in terms of ideals, convictions, mindset and culture, among all ethnic groups[9]. This line was set as an extension of the '14th Five-Year Plan for Economic and Social Development and Long-range Objectives Through the Year 2035 of the People's Republic of China'[10] held a few months earlier, which stated that 'The quality and level of

6 Although the Dongxiang people have used the Arabic script to write comments regarding religious matters, it has never been largely used among the Dongxiang population.

7 <https://www.gov.cn/xinwen/2021-08/28/content_5633940.htm> (consulted on 15/11/2024).

8 以铸牢中华民族共同体意识为主线。

9 必须促进各民族广泛交往交流交融，促进各民族在理想、信念、情感、文化上的团结统一。

10 中华人民共和国国民经济和社会发展第十四个五年规划和2035年远景目标纲要。<https://www.gov.cn/xinwen/2021-03/13/content_5592681.htm> (consulted on 15/11/2024).

education in ethnic minority areas will be improved, and efforts to promote the national common language and writing system will be increased'[11]. In the same spirit, following the constitution review and decision stating by the Legislative Affairs Commission of the National People's Congress Standing Committee in 2020 that regulations requiring schooling in the medium of minority languages were unconstitutional, the immediate effect of this decision on the ground was a switch to teaching certain school subjects in Putonghua (Standard Modern Chinese) in certain regions of Northern China (see Grey, forthcoming 2025 for details).

Other national Policies that impact the linguistic landscape of the Dongxiang people are not always necessarily linguistic ones. For example, the current National rural revitalisation plan (国家乡村振兴局) states that '*Teachers shall insist on using Putonghua to communicate with young children, encouraging them to speak Putonghua boldly in their daily lives and in games, and creating an environment in which they can communicate in Putonghua daily*.'[12] As a result, poverty eradication also serves as a tool for promoting Standard Chinese (see Grey forthcoming 2025 for details).

In the context of these reforms, the effects of the policies implemented had a direct and almost immediate impact on the proficiency and the transmission of the Dongxiang language among children. Between November 2019 and August 2023 – two of my latest visits in the area – the language shift to Standard Chinese had gained considerable ground, and younger speakers aged below 12 in 2023 already communicated with their peers and elders using only Standard Chinese, even if the latter addressed them in their own dialect or language. It is worth noting that the eldest of these children spoke fluent Dongxiang before the implementation of the law, but are now relucted to speak it.

Whereas in the early 2010s, the Dongxiang people viewed their language with little cultural interest – even with disdain, sometimes – they are now concerned that it may disappear in the decades to come. Indeed, Dongxiang is now a highly endangered language, and I believe that, if the language shift

---

11 提高民族地区教育质量和水平，加大国家通用语言文字推广力度。

12 教师坚持使用普通话与幼儿交流，鼓励幼儿在日常生活和游戏中大胆说普通话，营造用普通话日常交流的环境。

continues at this rate, language transmission will be completely over within the next 15 years. Consequently, it is important to emphasise here that this study reflects the data and results collected at that time (2009 and 2010), and that if a new sociolinguistic study were conducted today, the results would be thoroughly different. This study offers a 'snapshot' of a sociolinguistic situation that no longer exists, but which reflects a time at the edge of these linguistic changes. Because of the drastic developments that occurred in the Dongxiang Autonomous County, the data made available in this study cannot be reconstructed, and there are no other records of it. Thus, in order to comprehend the language shift that is currently happening, it is vital to understand what the situation was before changes were initiated.

For clarity purposes and ease for the readers, this book has been translated using the present of narration, but the events described refer to those of 2009 and 2010.

Photo 1: City centre of Suonanba, 2009.
On this picture, the main buildings of the Dongxiang Autonoumous County back at the time can be seen, including the Hotel of the minorities, which is the building on the right. The middle buildings are those of the administration and the staff's residences.

Photo 2: City centre of Suonanba, 2018.
The same picture taken from the same angle, 10 years after the first one. All buildings have been destroyed and rebuilt. The stadium has been filled with earth and concrete to raise up the level of the land.

Photo 3: Dongxiang woman and her sheep, Suonanba, 2018.
On this picture, it can be seen a Dongxiang woman leading her sheep to the pasture, reflecting the traditional way of life of Dongxiang.

Photo 4: Suonanba main market street, 2014.
This is where the main trade and commerce activities were taking place before the development of the new centre and the commercial area.

Photo 5: People's square and the Dongxiang Museum, Suonanba, 2024.
This kind of structures have been installed in almost all district capitals across China. The core values of the Chinese nation (white characters), and the Chinese communist party's symbol above slogan 'Chinese dream' on the right side can be seen.

Photo 6: Statue of 'Milagahei' illustrating Dongxiang people's folk culture, Park of culture, Suonanba, 2018.
Milagahei is a popular story among the Dongxiang people which has been chosen as a representation of their culture.

Photo 7: Primary school classroom in the village of Beiling, 2014.

Photo 8: Primary school classroom in Suonanba, 2018.
Between 2016 and 2018, all rural schools have been modernised with digital devices and internet access in order for the teacher to difuse contents in Standard Chinese directly in the classrooms.

Photo 9: Mosque, Narisi, 2023.

Photo 10: Muslim memorial in Tangwang, 2024.

Photo 11: Village of Maomao and the road to access to it, 2009.

Photo 12: Two Dongxiang men walking on the road from Suonanba to Linxia, 2010.

Photo 13: Daban's new developed city, 2023.

Photo 14: View of the Dongxiang mountains from the edge of Suonanba, 2018.

Photo 15: Village of Baihe, 2009.

Photo 16: Children on the road to Maomao village, 2010.

Photo 17: Entrance doors of a traditional house, Suonanba, 2009.

Photo 18: Traditional house, Suonanba, 2009.

Acknowledgements

This study is the culmination of the research that I conducted at the Ecole des hautes études en sciences sociales (EHESS), the results of which were presented in the doctoral thesis that I defended in 2012. This work is based on that thesis, which has since been restructured and now contains a certain amount of updated information.

This thesis has been prepared as part of the project entitled 'Language Contact and Linguistic Changes: the case of Chinese and Altaic languages in North-western China', a National Research Agency (ANR) project presented by the East Asian Language Research Centre (CRLAO) – UMR 8563 of the CNRS – 131 Boulevard Saint-Michel, 75005 Paris, and the project entitled 'Languages in Contact in North-western China: Convergence, Mixed Languages or Linguistic Area?', presented by the Chiang Ching-kuo Foundation for International Scholarly Exchange, Taipei, Taiwan (Project CCK-F–RG011-U-07).

The thesis initially comprised two parts, one dealing with sociolinguistics and the other with linguistic description, illustrating the languages in contact and the impact of Chinese in Dongxiang. The second part, having already been published in French in 2022[13], this work concerns itself primarily with the sociolinguistic context of Dongxiang.

This study has been translated from French to English thanks to the INALCO Translation Grant 2023 by Adrian Boyle, CertTrans MCIL.

---

13 "Contact de langues et changements linguistiques en dongxiang" [Language contact and linguistic change in Dongxiang], Cahiers de Linguistique Asie Orientale 17, 2022, (225 p).

Notes on the Transcriptions

For the transcriptions in Dongxiang, I have used the alphabet created by Ma and Chen (2001) in the *Dunxian kielien khidei kielien kieleni lvgeqi* [Dongxiang-Chinese dictionary]. This alphabet uses the *Hanyu pinyin fang'an* 汉语拼音方案, the pinyin transcription of Chinese, as a basis for developing the Dongxiang transcription. The Chinese diphthongs represented in pinyin as *ia*, *ie* and *iao* are transcribed in Dongxiang as *ya*, *ye* and *yao*, when they appear at the beginning of a word. The Chinese diphthongs represented in pinyin as *ua*, *ui* and *uai* are transcribed in Dongxiang as *wa*, *wi* and *wai*, when they appear at the beginning of a word.

The correspondences between the Dongxiang '*pinyin*' alphabetical transcriptions and the International Phonetic Alphabet (IPA, in square brackets) are shown in Table 1:

Table 1: Correspondences between Dongxiang *pinyin* transcription and API

a	[a]	ie	[iə]	t	[t]	j	[dʑ]
e	[ə]	iu	[iu]	n	[n]/ [ŋ]	q	[tɕ]
i	[i]	ua	[ua]	l	[l]	x	[ɕ]
ii	[ɯ]	ui	[ui]	r	[r]	zh	[dʐ]
o	[o]	iao	[iao]	g	[g]	ch	[tʂ]
u	[u]	uai	[uai]	j	[k]	sh	[ʂ]
ai	[ai]	b	[b]	gh	[ɢ]	z	[dz]

ei	[əi]	p	[p]	kh	[q]	c	[ts]
ao	[ao]	m	[m]	h	[χ]	s	[s]
ou	[əu]	f	[f]	gv	[ʁ]	w	[w]
ia	[ia]	d	[d]	hh	[h]	y	[j]

As this system does not differentiate between open and closed final nasals, I have included a 'vowel + *ng*' transcription to denote closed finals (even though these are still represented as 'vowel + *n*' in the dictionary).

List of Abbreviations

Languages and Geography

DX	Dongxiang
KH	Khalkha
LX	Linxia
MMON	Middle Mongolian

Literary References

HYYY	*Huayi yiyu* (Sino-Barbarian dictionary)
SHM	*Secret History of the Mongols* (*Mongolin nuuts tovchoo*)
LXFY	*Linxia Fangyan* – see bibliography
XDHYCD	*Xiandai Hanyu Cidian* (A Dictionary of Current Chinese) – see bibliography

Linguistic abbreviations

1	1st person singular
1LOG	logophoric 1st person singular
2	2nd person singular
3	3rd person singular
1PL	1st person plural
2PL	2nd person plural
3PL	3rd person plural
3REFL	3rd person reflexive

ACC	accusative (case)
BVA	borrowed verb auxiliary
CAUS	causative
CL	classifier
COND	conditional (converb)
COP	copula
CSL	causal (converb)
DAT	dative (case)
DEM	demonstrative
DEG	degree
GEN	genitive (case)
GRD	gerundive
IPFV	imperfective (aspect)
INT	integrative (converb)
LOC	locative (case)
MAN	manner
MP	modal particle
NMLZ	nominaliser (nominal derivative)
NEG	negation
PL	plural
PST	past (tense)
PFV	perfective (aspect)
POSS	possessive
POT	potential
PROG	progressive (converb)
PURP	purposive (converb)
QUOT	quotative (converb)
REFL	reflexive
RES	resultative
SEM	switch event marker (converb)
SEQ	sequential (converb)
SIM	simultaneity (converb)
SUB	subordination marker
SIM	simultaneous (converb)
SUB	subordinating
SS	successive (converb)

Introduction

The Dongxiang language (ISO 639-3), spoken by the people of the homonymous ethnic group (known in Chinese as *Dōngxiāng zú* 东乡族), is one of the Mongolic languages referred to as 'peripheral', and belongs to the Shirongol group[14] that also includes the Bonan, Mangghuer, Mongghul, Mongghuor[15] and Eastern Yugur (or Shira Yugur) languages. These languages share the particularity of having been isolated from other Mongolic languages, and feature common typological elements inherited from Middle Mongolian. Furthermore, they have all been influenced by the surrounding languages, which have caused the modifications and linguistic features specific to this group. These languages are spoken in the border region between Gansu and Qinghai, known as the Hexi Corridor (河西走廊)[16]. There are also several other distinctive ethnic groups that speak languages particular to this region but belonging to different linguistic groups. Furthermore, the Chinese, Tibetan, Turkic and Mongolic languages spoken here have been in contact with one another, thus creating the region's unique dynamic. All of these languages have influenced each other to such an extent that researchers

14 See Janhunen (2003b) for a definition of the Shirongolic languages.

15 Mangghuer, Mongghul and Mongghuor were initially grouped together under the term "Monguor language" by De Smedt and Mostaert (1933) but what their work actually detailed was the Mongghul language; Schröder (1952; 1959–1970; 1964) and Todaeva (1973) distinguished a second variety: Mongghuor. More recently, Slater (2003) distinguished the Mangghuer variety and advocated for its status as an independent language (see Janhunen in Schram, 1957, reis. Stuart, 2006).

16 This term is a reference to a historic route that was part of the Silk Road.

consider the region to be a *Sprachbund* or "linguistic area": Dwyer (1992) speaks of the 'Northwest China Sprachbund', Slater (2003) of the 'Qinghai-Gansu Sprachbund' and Janhunen et al. (2004) of the "Amdo Sprachbund".

The Muslim Dongxiang people are mainly concentrated in Dongxiang County, situated in a mountainous region that remained isolated for several centuries. The Dongxiang language has been influenced significantly by Linxia (临夏话 *línxià huà*), a Chinese dialect spoken in the nearby city of the same name. Linxia, more generally considered to be the dialect spoken in the region of this city, is known in China as the Hezhou (河洲话 *Hézhōu huà*) regional dialect. Whilst the latter is indisputably a Chinese dialect, its classification is an issue of ongoing debate, as this variety displays certain linguistic characteristics that demonstrate influence by language contact, particularly with the other Mongolic languages of the region. The Dongxiang people, owing to both their geographical isolation and their determination to remain apart from non-Muslim communities, were denied contact with speakers of other varieties of Chinese over a very long period of time. However, since the late twentieth century, Dongxiang County has seen a significant urban and social transformation, brought on by economic development. The origins of this development can be found in the policies of reform and openness[17] introduced by the government from the late 1970s, the effects of which did not begin to have an impact in Dongxiang County until the end of the 1990s. This development is marked today by new contacts between populations, and thus between languages, which has led to the emergence of new linguistic practices that can be observed in a part of the population. Mobility, the growing use of new technologies and the development of education are among the factors arising from this social transformation, and have led to a broadening of language contacts which had, for a long time, been almost exclusively with Linxia. Various dialects of the northwest Mandarin group, including Lanzhou (*Lánzhōu huà* 兰州话) and *Putonghua* (*Pǔtōnghuà* 普通话), the standard form of Chinese, are thus now appearing in the speech of certain people, notably among younger speakers.

Interest in the Dongxiang language, among both Western and Eastern researchers, only began in the second half of the twentieth century. The first concise descriptions of Dongxiang were published by Todaeva (1961)

[17] 改革开放 *gǎigé kāifàng* in Chinese.

and Nasunbayar (1961). Since the 1980s, other researchers have studied the language with renewed interest; Liu (1983), Buhe (1986), and Kim (2003) provide slightly more detailed descriptions of the main linguistic features of Dongxiang. The principal compilation of linguistic material in Dongxiang was published by Buhe (1987). To date, the work of Field (1997) remains the most complete, providing us with a highly detailed linguistic description and highlighting those phonological and lexical elements influenced by language contacts. Bao (2006), whose work focussed on language contact-induced phenomena, also described changes in the Dongxiang language, but without taking into consideration the specificities of the various Chinese dialects and with very little detail on the linguistic environment of the Dongxiang. While descriptions and compilations of texts in the Dongxiang language have increased in number since the mid-twentieth century, studies of the social environment of the Dongxiang are rare (Chen 2006) and there have thus far been no sociolinguistic studies.

I therefore considered it important to report on language-contact-related linguistic changes as observed in contemporary Dongxiang. These linguistic changes have developed gradually, as a result of enduring contacts that have brought about radical, permanent changes to the language. Today, these contacts are different in nature and arise less gradually, in parallel with the intensification of contacts with new dialects, resulting in changes that respond to emerging phenomena and reflect a state of flux. Given that the Dongxiang community is largely bilingual, and that language contact is inevitable owing to contacts between speakers, these phenomena thus imply a social reality that is important to describe, in order to understand the mechanisms that have caused and continue to cause these changes in the Dongxiang language.

This study comprises six chapters, profiling the sociolinguistic situation of Dongxiang. Chapter 2 covers the historical, geographical and social elements that facilitate an understanding of the general context of the Dongxiang language. Chapter 3 covers the general linguistic context of the Dongxiang language, including its place within the Mongolic family and the other Mongolic languages spoken in the Gansu-Qinghai area. Chapter 4 outlines the situation as it stood at the time of the study (2009–2010) and, through use of a synchronic approach, enables the description and analysis of the relationships that exist between the languages in contact within the Dongxiang community and of linguistic representations (Chapter 5). Chapter 6 provides an overview of Contact-Induced Change in the Dongxiang language.

Currently available materials and studies remain sporadic. In his 2006 study, Chen considers the question of the Dongxiang community from a social perspective, focussing more on historical, geographical and, to a certain extent, anthropological elements. He only addresses the language issue superficially. When compared with the study of certain other languages of the Gansu-Qinghai region, it is only recently that researchers have started to take an interest in the Dongxiang language. The Russian researcher Todaeva (1961) was the first to publish a sample of vocabulary, and it was not until the 1980s that Chinese researchers renewed their interest in the language. In 1984, Buhe compiled and transcribed a body of material in Dongxiang, which he published in 1987; this was the first corpus of its type, comprising 49 texts of varying length. These texts are organised into seven chapters: (1) Translated everyday phrases, (2) Translated long stories, (3) Popular, traditional stories, (4) Nursery rhymes, (5) Proverbs, (6) Riddles, and (7) Popular traditions and customs. As indicated by their titles, the first two chapters comprise collections of phrases and texts translated from Chinese. Each text features three lines: the first, a transcription of the Dongxiang phrase using the International Phonetic Alphabet; the second, a word-for-word transcription of the elements of the first phrase in *hudum* Mongolian alphabet; and finally, the third line is the Chinese translation of the Dongxiang phrase. This transcription methodology allows us to easily spot Dongxiang words of Mongolic origin and, to a certain extent, to understand their etymology. The Dongxiang language material collected by Buhe provides a solid foundation for analysis. However, no details are provided about the circumstances of the study and, given that it is not a corpus of spontaneous speech but, for the most part, a translated corpus, its utility is somewhat limited. Indeed, one could also question the extent to which the original Chinese texts may have influenced the translation into Dongxiang. Furthermore, a number of standard phrases, reflecting the communist ideology of the time, were inserted into the texts, increasing the number of Chinese elements, especially at the lexical level. The unpublished study by Kenneth Field (1997), conducted as part of his doctoral research, along with that of Bao (2006), use Buhe's corpus as the primary source for their analyses.

Given the lack of recent, comprehensive material, it seemed clear that there was a need for a sociolinguistic survey to be conducted and for a new language corpus to be collected. I therefore conducted two field surveys, from March to July 2009 and from March to July 2010. This work will report on the results of the sociolinguistic survey and analysis that took place primarily during the first of these periods. The linguistic description of the contact-induced changes is available in Lefort (2022). Conducting the two surveys allowed me to visit the villages of Daban 达板, Wangji 王集, Suonanba 锁南坝, Beiling 北岭, Longquan 龙泉, Dongling 东岭, Baihe 百和, Heishishan 黑石山, Maomao 毛毛, Nalesi 那勒寺, Yanling 沿岭 Dongling 董岭, Zhaojia 赵家, and Macheng 马城 (cf. Map 2).

While conducting the sociolinguistic survey, I was accompanied by Axiye, a Dongxiang speaker in her thirties who did not know her exact date of birth. The survey was conducted among a larger number of women than men for two reasons. First, at the time I was visiting the villages, the men were often absent from the home for reasons of work. Second, being a woman myself, it was easier to establish connections with other women than with men, for social, cultural and religious reasons.

Furthermore, indifference towards this study posed a major challenge at the time of the survey. As a matter of fact, as most of the speakers questioned were suffering from particularly severe economic insecurity, they had very little interest in answering linguistic questions, and could see no pragmatic purpose in the project. Also, given the very low level of education among the respondents, most did not understand the nature of the study being conducted. Additionally, as a foreigner and a non-Muslim, it was very difficult for me to convince respondents that I had not been commissioned by the Communist Party to gather personal information about them. Indeed, the villages we visited were sometimes so remote that outsiders would only travel to them to take part in family gatherings (weddings, funerals, etc.) or for official purposes (birth rate surveys, censuses, etc.). Therefore, I most often introduced myself as a foreign journalist, in order to facilitate access to the families. However, this approach led to confusion regarding the aims of the survey among respondents, who often wanted to reorientate their testimony towards information relating to their daily lives and their economic insecurity.

General Context

2.1 Historical Context and Origin of the Dongxiang Group

2.1.1 History of Dongxiang

Gansu province and the region in which the present-day Dongxiang County is situated have, since ancient times, been areas of significant ethnic intermingling. Furthermore, their borders have been redrawn throughout their history, with control of them passing between various Chinese authorities and populations labelled as 'barbarians'[18].

The region in which present-day Dongxiang is situated is known to have been a place in which the Qiang 羌 were active since at least the era of the Warring States (475–221 BCE) and formed the most westerly region of the Qin Kingdom. The Chinese term Qiang, along with its associated character, alludes to the populations of the Amdo region of the present-day Qinghai province and, according to Schram (1957), means 'sheep farmers'. However, from an ethnolinguistic perspective, very little historical information on these populations has survived, apart from the fact that they were not Chinese (Janhunen 2006).

During the Qin dynasty (221–206 BCE), Dongxiang was integrated into the Duchy of Longxi 陇西, located in the Baohan 枹罕 district. It returned

18 To describe the populations of non-Chinese origin peoples in the outer reaches of the empire, the Chinese used various terms linked to their geographical location, with no reference to the tribal names the people gave themselves. These terms include *yí* 夷, *mán* 蛮, *róng* 戎, *dí* 狄, often translated as 'barbarians' in western literature. See Liu (2004), for example.

to the hands of the Qiang during the Western Han period (206 BCE–25 CE) but became part of the Chinese empire once again and was reintegrated into the Duchy of Longxi at the beginning of the Eastern Han dynasty (25–200)[19].

Then, in 214, during the time of the Three Kingdoms (220–280), Cao Cao 曹操 (155–220) sent his troops into the Duchy, which then came under the command of the Wei state (Chen 2006: 26).

During the period of the Sixteen Kingdoms (304–439), Dongxiang became the theatre for a succession of wars between the various kingdoms and, within a century, passed successively into the hands of the Former Zhao (304–329), the Former Liang (320–376), the Later Zhao (319–351), the Former Qin (351–394), the Later Qin (384–417) and the Western Qin (385–431). Moreover, the population suffered near annihilation as the natural environment fell into significant decline. It should be mentioned that Zhang Jun 张骏, one of the most important figures of the Former Liang era and the highest-ranking officer of the dynasty, established himself in Hezhou 河州, modern-day Linxia 临夏, in 335. His authority extended from Jincheng 金城, now known as Lanzhou 兰州, to Hanzhong 汉中, situated in modern-day Shaanxi. The current Dongxiang region was under the administrative control of Hezhou.

In the early 520s, the Tuyuhun 吐谷浑, or A-zha in Tibetan[20], moved from what is now the Qinghai region and seized the region of Hezhou 河州, putting Dongxiang under their control (Li 2007).

At the start of the Sui dynasty (581–618), Emperor Wendi 文帝 (541–604) established his prefecture in Lanzhou, incorporating Dongxiang into it. Once the region had been completely pacified, the Linxia County borders that we know today were established.

In 672, during the Tang dynasty (618–907), the Tubo 吐番 crushed the Tuyuhun still present in the region and took control of Hezhou, where they remained for almost a century before control of the territory returned to the empire (Cai 2007). In 866, they were conquered themselves, not by the Tang, but by the Uyghur tribes, a Turkic people from Central Asia who were established in Huangzhong and who swore allegiance to the Chinese empire (Schram 1957).

---

19 See de Crespigny (1984).

20 Probably descendants of the Xianbei 鲜卑, an ethnic proto-Mongolic people originating in the east of modern-day Mongolia and also known as *Sienpi* or *Syanbi* in western literature (Schram 1957).

From the end of the Tang dynasty until the beginning of the Song (960–1279), and including the period of the Five Dynasties (c. 907–960), Hezhou was dominated more or less continuously by the Tubo. At the beginning of the Song, Hezhou was controlled by the grandsons of Gusiluo 唃斯罗, a descendant of the Tubo, who governed the region for around 100 years (Chen 2006). Then, in 1047, the region was reclaimed by the Song, who established the Xihe Road[21] 熙河路 there, in what is now Lintao County 临洮, of which modern-day Dongxiang is a part. However, control of northern China quickly fell once again into the hands of the "barbarians". The north and the Hezhou regions were thus now bordering the empires of the Jin 金 (1115–1234), a Jurchen people (*Nüzhen* 女真 in Chinese) of Manchurian origin, and the Xixia 西夏 (1038–1227), ethnic Tibetans known to the Mongols as *tangγud* (Tanguts). The Jin spoke a Tungusic language (or, according to Janhunen 2003a, a para-Mongolic language), and the Tanguts a Tibeto-Burman language.

Under the Yuan 元 (1206–1368), the Tanguts were defeated by the Mongols, who pushed them back into Tibet as the former Huangzhong border region became depopulated (Shram 1957). A large number of Mongol generals and their army were sent to this region. They established three counties there: Qiang 羌, Ninghe 宁合 and Anxiang 安乡, of which modern-day Dongxiang forms a part. Hezhou was then turned into a garrison (河州卫 *Hézhōu wèi*) and later became the prefecture of Lintao (临洮府 *Líntáo fǔ*).

It was during the Ming dynasty (1368–1644) that the region was given the name "Dongxiang". Hezhou was the administrative capital of the garrison of the same name, which was divided administratively into four parts centred around Hezhou, with the modern-day Dongxiang Autonomous County situated to the east (东 *dōng*) of Hezhou, giving it its name (*dōng xiāng*, lit. 'village of the east'). From this period, until that of the Qing (1368–1911), Dongxiang remained under the administrative government of Hezhou, before returning to the control of Lanzhou at the beginning of the Qing dynasty.

During the time of the Republic of China (1912–1949), Hezhou was renamed Daohe 导河 and the modern-day county of Dongxiang was divided into four parts: the counties of Daohe, Hezheng 和政, Ningding 宁定 and Yongjing 永靖.

---

21 The term 'road', 路 lù in Chinese, refers to a primary-level administrative subdivision, and was introduced during the Northern Song dynasty by Emperor Taizu.

In 1950, the People's Republic of China established the Dongxiang Autonomous County (*Dōngxiāngzú zìzhì xiàn* 东乡族自治县), the borders of which have not changed since. It forms part of the Linxia Hui Autonomous Prefecture (*Línxià Huízú zìzhìqū* 临夏回族自治区). It is only since this time that research into the established population of the county and its language has really begun.

2.1.2 The origins of the population

The Dongxiang, along with speakers of other Mongolic languages in the Gansu-Qinghai region, the Monguor (*tǔzú* 土族), the Bonan (*bǎo'ānzú* 保安 族) and the Yugur (*yùgǔzú* 裕固族), live geographically distant from the speakers of other Mongolic languages, who are found predominantly in Mongolia (i.e., Outer Mongolia), Inner Mongolia (*Nèiménggǔ* 内蒙古), Chinese Xinjiang and the Republic of Buryatia[22]. Researchers have speculated about the history and origins of the Dongxiang, proposing several hypotheses.

In the first half of the twentieth century, the most widespread hypothesis among Chinese researchers[23], was that of the Mongol origin of the Dongxiang. They based their analysis primarily on linguistic criteria. Indeed, a large proportion of Dongxiang vocabulary is of Mongol origin, and certain syntactic elements make it possible to establish a direct link with Middle Mongolian (thirteenth–fourteenth centuries)[24]. Furthermore, these researchers consider there to be cultural similarities between the Dongxiang and Mongols (felt making, dietary habits, etc.) that enable the two populations to be linked. However, these traditions are found in many Central Asian cultures and are not exclusive to the Mongols. More recently, Dai Yuhing and Yang Dongya[25] (1991) supported this hypothesis, albeit it with some degree of nuance, arguing that other populations, such as the Hui 回, the Han 汉[26] and perhaps the

---

22 The Kalmyk speakers found along the river Volga in the Russian Federation, and the Moghol speakers concentrated in Afghanistan, are the most geographically distant from the central hub.

23 See Ma Guozhong and Ma Zixiang (1982: 60).

24 See Chapter 2.

25 Cited by Ma and Wang (2003: 32).

26 The Hui, a Muslim people, are one of the 55 official ethnic minorities in the People's Republic of China. The Han are the ethnic majority in China, representing around 92% of the current Chinese population. They are sometimes considered to be

Tibetans (藏), had probably contributed to the creation of the ethnic group. However, even if the relationship between Dongxiang and Middle Mongolian offers proof of contacts and probably of common heritage between the two languages, it offers no evidence of a genetic relationship between the two ethnic groups.

In the 1980s several researchers, including Ma and Ma (1982), suggested that the Dongxiang may have descended from the Muslim *Huihui Semu* (回回色目) populations of Central Asia, who were conscripted into Genghis Khan's armies and then deported to the Dongxiang region in around 1227. These clues do not help us establish beyond doubt the origins of the Dongxiang, but do nonetheless indicate to which group they may have belonged in the era of Mongol domination. The term *Huihui Semu* means "Muslims of all origins" (*sèmù* 色目 being the abbreviation of *gèsè míngmù* 各色名目 lit. 'of all categories'[27]) and thus describes a category of people at a defined moment in history and not a specific ethnic group.

In his work, Li (1983) briefly develops the hypothesis that the Dongxiang may be of Shatuo 沙陀 (or Saltu, or Salto) origin, that is, a Turkic group descended from the Chigil tribes, who were part of one of the six Chu tribes of the Yueban Kingdom[28] and who took refuge in China in 808. This hypothesis is based mainly on a phonological reconstruction of the word *santa* (**salto > *sangto > *santo > santa*), a term used by the Dongxiang to describe themselves, and also on the fact that some researchers allege a link between the Shatuo and the Qinghai Monguors (Schram 1957). Given the phonological transformations in Dongxiang[29], and the links that can be established with Middle Mongolian, this reconstruction seems somewhat implausible. However, the author bases this theory on other historical elements which may confirm the Turkic origin of the Dongxiang, but not necessarily their *shalto* (or *shatuo*) origin. It should be noted that, according to Zuev (1960), the term *shatuo* corresponds to the Sanskrit *sart*, thus corroborating the hypothesis, predominant since the 1980s, of the *Sarta* origin of the Dongxiang.

representatives of the 'historical' Chinese people descended from the ancient Huaxia (华夏民族 Huáxià mínzú) ethnic group.

27 Lipman (1997).

28 See Gumilev (1988).

29 See Chapter 6.

Indeed, the idea of the *Sarta* origin of the Dongxiang, that is according to Grousset (1939), a population originating in the Khwarezmian Empire[30] (1077–1231), is dominant in China today. This idea had, moreover, been mooted in the West since the late 1940s, first by Moestaert (1947) and then by Poppe (1955a). Ma and Ma (1982) were the first in China to consider it, followed by Ma (1983), who took it further by drawing a parallel between the words *Sarta* and *Santa*. It is based on both a phonological reconstruction using Middle Mongolian (*sarta* > **sangta* > *santa*) and historical elements. The most recent studies, from the early 1990s (Ma 1992) attempt to add new elements by drawing on comparative studies of blood groups and DNA (Xie et al. 2002). These studies, however, are less than satisfactory, given that the sampling was only conducted among the residents of a single village, representing around 150 individuals.

It is, in fact, highly likely that the term *santa* is related to the word *sart* (*sǎ ěr tǎ* 撒尔塔 in Chinese), often used in thirteenth-century Mongolian texts. Furthermore, it is also found in writings on the history of this period[31] and in texts written in Persian, such as *The History of the World Conqueror*[32], in which this term is defined as designating a people of Central Asia (Hangin 1973), most likely from the Khwarezmian Empire, a Muslim people composed mainly of merchants. Grousset (1944) also mentions that in 1219, as the Conqueror was preparing his expedition against the Sultan of Khwarezm, he requested auxiliaries from the Tangut sovereign, addressing him with these words: 'Thou has said, "I shall be [thy] right hand", My "golden tether" being broken by the Sarta'ul (the Sultan of Khwarezm), I have set forth to take account of [him]. Set [thou] forth, being [my] right hand'[33]. E'erdengtai (1980: 235) attributes several meanings to the term Sarta in the *Secret History of the Mongols*[34]: (1) Central Asian people, (2) Traders, (3) An Altaï clan and (4)

---

30 Grousset (1939: 296) writes 'in the Secret History of the Mongols, the Khwarezmians are referred to as the Sarta'ul'.

31 *Mongγol-un niγuca tobčiyan* [Secret History of the Mongols] (mid-thirteenth century); *Köke sudur* [The Blue Chronicle], Injannasi, nineteenth century.

32 *Ta'rikh-i Jahan-Gusha* [The History of the World Conqueror], written in Persian between 1252 and 1259 by Ata-Malek Juvaini, also known in Chinese as Zhi Feini 志费尼, describes the conquest of Persia by the Mongols.

33 Grousset (1944: 417); English translation of quote taken from Francis Woodman Cleaves (1982: 198).

34 Ibidem.

All people living in the towns and cities of Central Asia. Dawson (1980) also believes that the meaning of the word Sarta had already evolved by the thirteenth century and no longer referred only to a specific ethnicity, but also had the meaning of 'Muslims' in general. Finally, Lattimore (in the introduction to Schram 1957, reis. Stuart 2006: 89) states that 'their [the Sarta'ul] ancestors were of the Turkic-speaking, mainly Muslim Central Asian people whom the Mongols called "Sart". In this sense the Mongol use (in the form Sarta'ul) is recorded as early as the "Stone of Chingis Khan," dating from about 1225'.

Furthermore, in Dongxiang the term *santa* describes not only their own group, but also applies to the ensemble of Muslim populations in the region, including the Hui, which accords with the meaning of *sarta* in Middle Mongolian. Schram (1957), in describing a local general from the Monguors region, states that this individual differentiated between the various ethic groups of the area, and that both the Tibetans and the Monguors used the term *santa* to refer to the groups of Mongolic origin that had converted to Islam. Additionally, in the *Monguor Dictionary*[35] compiled by Mostaert and De Smedt (1933)[36], the word *santa* refers not only to the people living east of the Taohe River, but is also defined as being the "name that, according to Potanin, the Shirongol of Pao Nan give to the Salar Turks, who are also of the Muslim religion". This would suggest that the term is used to refer not only to the Dongxiang, but in fact to all the Muslim groups in the region, be they of Mongolic, Turkic or Chinese origin.

Furthermore, historical information shows that, between the time that Genghis Khan's troops crossed the Irtysh in 1219, to conquer the Khwarezmian Empire, and the conquest of Xi Xia in 1227[37], the Mongols deported the populations of the conquered towns in Central Asia in their tens of thousands, particularly their artisans, to the four corners of the empire, including the regions of present-day Gansu (Morgan 1986; Ma 1992). The Dongxiang region still bears traces of this Mongol occupation and, even today, some villages have retained names that reflect the activities

35 The Mongolic language of the peripheral group, spoken in Qinghai. Nowadays, two linguistic groups are recognised: Mangghuer and Mongghul. See Section 2.3.

36 *Monguor Dictionary*, p. 324.

37 There were several Mongol invasions between 1227 and 1253, resulting in the Mongols taking administrative control of the Tibetan kingdom.

of artisans and military personnel. In their oral tradition, the Dongxiang recall that two *Sarta* Muslim missionaries, Hamuze 哈木则 and Alyad 阿里阿答, came to Hezhou during the Ming dynasty to preach Sufism. They are thought to have come to convert their kinfolk, who had settled there a few centuries earlier (Chen 2006).

From a linguistic point of view, the Dongxiang language contains a specific Turkic vocabulary, of which some terms predate the thirteenth century (Field 1997). These correspond either to borrowings integrated very early into the language or to a substrate of the original language of the Dongxiang. This would indicate that the Dongxiang had close relations with the Turks or that they were of Turkic origin. In the latter case, they would have experienced a language shift, a mechanism whereby the members of a community abandon their original vernacular language in favour of another.

Whether from a linguistic, social or religious perspective, the *sarta* origin of the Dongxiang appears most likely, and it is possible that they are a population of mixed origin. Indeed, after the conquest of Xi Xia, the artisan populations, by their nature itinerant men, must not have completely severed relations with their Mongol, Tibetan and Han Chinese neighbours; they certainly connected with them through inter-ethnic marriages. As I mentioned above, the neighbouring regions of southeast Gansu and southwest Qinghai include other Mongolic languages classified in the same group of so-called "peripheral" languages. The speakers of those languages may have had origins linked to those of the Dongxiang.

2.2 Modern Context

2.2.1 Demographic and geographic aspects

According to the Sixth National Population Census[38] of 2010, the Dongxiang population totals 513,803 individuals across the whole of China, of which 451,622, or 87.9% of the total, are in Gansu. The Dongxiang are mainly concentrated in Dongxiang Autonomous County, where they totaled around 291,600[39]. According to the Seventh National Population Census, the total

---

38 There being no more recent official studies, we will use these figures for the purposes of this study.

39 *Statistical Bulletin on the Economic and Social Situation of Dongxiang Autonomous County*, Gansu Bureau of Statistics, 2011 [accessed 08/07/2015].

population of Dongxiang was 290,034 people. Another part of the community, representing around 21,900 individuals, is likewise settled in Jishishan Bonan, Dongxiang and Salar Autonomous County in Gansu, and a further 44,000 or so individuals are settled in the counties of Yining and Huocheng, situated in Yili Kazakh Autonomous Prefecture in Xinjiang.

Approximately, 87.4% of the county's total population identifies as 'ethnically' Dongxiang, which equates to 42% of the total Dongxiang population of China and 48% of the Dongxiang population of Gansu Province. The rest of the population is made up of Hui (2.92% of the county's population, or 11,537 people) and Han (9.92% or 31,364 people); the remaining 0.1% are from other ethnic groups, including Salar.

Since 2004, the county has been organised into five large market towns (镇 *zhèn*) – Suonanba 锁南坝, Daban 达板, Hetan 河滩, Nalesi[40] 那勒寺, Tangwang 唐汪 – and nineteen townships (乡 *xiāng*), covering a total area of 1,467 km^2.

According to the 2010 national census figures, 95.66% of the population was rural at the time, the other 4.34% living in the towns. Compared to the data from 2000, the town-dwelling population has grown by 2.1% and the agricultural workforce constitutes 50.30% of the total population. Approximately, 53.82% of the population live in mountainous areas, of which 45.28% are agricultural workers (Li 2007). Cultivable agricultural land represents only 16.2% of the total area, with 90% of this being in mountainous areas. Severe droughts render the land less productive, forcing the inhabitants of these areas to disperse and move to the mountain slopes and ridges.

Until 2010, road networks were practically non-existent, leaving the population completely isolated and often with access to neither running water nor electricity. Since then, numerous roads have been built or restored, thereby opening up the county and its more inaccessible villages; a high-speed road, crossing Dongxiang County, now connects Lanzhou and Linxia. According to official authorities, all of the villages are now accessible by road[41].

Dongxiang County is surrounded by rivers: to the east by the Tao 洮, to the west by the Daxia 大夏, to the north by the Yellow River (which passes through the Liujia Gorge – 刘家峡), and to the south by the Baxie 巴谢. However, access to water in the areas located in the centre of the county

---

40 Also spelled Narisi 那日寺.

41 For further details, see the *Statistical Bulletin on the Economic and Social Situation of Dongxiang Autonomous County*, Gansu Bureau of Statistics, 2011.

remains very restricted owing to their high altitude, the highest plateau being at 2,605 m. The terrain here is very rugged, with over 90% of the land consisting of mountainous areas above 1,800 m in elevation. The county is part of the Loess Plateau zone. Average annual rainfall does not exceed 350 mm, and therefore, owing to the lack of water, drought conditions prevail for 93% of the year (Chen 2006). This state of drought is largely attributed to the land clearing and intensive tree felling that began early in the Ming dynasty (1368–1644), during the Dongxiang's transformation from a pastoral to an agrarian society. Indeed, once the trees had been cleared, the wind was able to circulate freely, causing aridity and the impoverishment of the cultivable soils. Furthermore, owing to the high altitude, the existing land irrigation systems were no solution to these issues. The climate is continental, with an average temperature of 4.9 degrees in the mountainous areas and 8 degrees in the riverine areas. During periods of drought, it is not unusual for other natural disasters, such as landslides, earthquakes or floods, to also occur.

The county's geographic typology is closely related to the distribution of its speakers; the closer a village is to the mountainous region of the centre, the lower its agricultural output will be, the worse its economic situation, and the greater its proportion of Dongxiang speakers. Conversely, if a village is located on the peripheries of the county, or close to a river, its economic situation is more likely to be better and the proportion of speakers of one of the varieties of Chinese will be higher.

2.2.2 Socio-economic aspects

Between 2000 and 2010, the Autonomous County experienced significant economic development, albeit on a more limited scale than the rest of China. The various sectors of activity have all grown significantly, but unevenly. In 2005, the primary sector accounted for 36.02% of total income from agricultural activities, and the secondary sector, 33.98%; whereas in 2012, the primary sector accounted for 32.48%, the secondary sector, 21.37%, and the tertiary sector, 46.15%. This demonstrates a sizeable decrease in industrial activities in favour of the service sector, and a significant diversification of economic activities within the county.

In 2009, the agricultural sector, comprising 96.40% of the active population, was still the principal activity, while the other sectors, including the commercial sector, represented only 3.6%. These figures correspond, respectively, to the rural and urban population percentages mentioned earlier.

Professional activities are still divided by ethnic origin. The Dongxiang and the Hui are primarily farmers, merchants, stockmen, restaurateurs and craftsmen, whereas the Han are farmers, stockmen and construction workers (Ma 2008).

Government aid programmes have multiplied since the 2000s, resulting in a significant increase in wages over 10 years. However, wages remain modest when compared to other Chinese agricultural regions. In 2000, 30.68% of the agricultural population had modest incomes (between 630 and 879 RMB monthly[42]), and 24.4% were below the poverty threshold (less than 600 RMB annually); the average monthly income of farmers increased from 1138 RMB in 2006, to 1419 RMB in 2008, and to 2062 RMB in 2010[43,44].

The mobile workforce in the Dongxiang area is composed largely of young men; this phenomenon differs appreciably from the rest of China, where the mobile rural workforce tends to be mixed. We have no figures concerning this workforce, as they have not featured in any studies; however, the Dongxiang population living outside the county boundaries has been the subject of a census, which is a significant and representative indicator of a possible work network organisation. This practice is not new since, from the Qing dynasty (1644–1911) onwards, a part of the Dongxiang population had emigrated to neighbouring counties. This phenomenon, which has intensified since the the major economic reforms of the 1980s[45], is increasingly prevalent. In 2000, 12.11% of the total Dongxiang population was living outwith the borders of Gansu, mainly in Xinjiang, Qinghai and Ningxia. 47.63% of Gansu's Dongxiang population were living in Dongxiang Autonomous County, with the remaining 56.47% being spread around the counties of Guanghe 广和, Hezheng 和政, Jishishan, Kangle 康乐, in the towns of Linxia, Yumen 玉门, Yongjing 永靖, Lanzhou and Anxi 安西. Between 1990 and 2000, the

42 Exchange rate in 2000: around 8.27 RMB = 1 USD.

43 Hu (2012).

44 Data taken from the sixth national census (2010).

45 Chinese Economic Reform (改革开放政策 *Gǎigé kāifàng zhèngcè*) refers to the programme of economic changes termed 'socialism with Chinese characteristics' in the People's Republic of China.

Dongxiang population of Jiuquan 酒泉 grew from 44 to 5,623, and that of Lanzhou from 148 to 1,456 (Ma and Zao 2005).

Zhou Linglang (2003) studied the specific case of the village of Muyeli 苜叶里, in an attempt to determine the factors that were encouraging men to leave for the cities as mobile workers. She concludes that workforce mobility is primarily related to family income and savings capacity. The number of farmworkers in a family can also be linked to workforce mobility: the more farmworkers there are in a family, the more likely they are to become mobile. Finally, the relationship between a family's net income and the cultivable area of a plot of land also enters the equation. The larger a family's cultivable land, the greater its income. Therefore, migrating to an urban setting in order to pursue non-agricultural work may represent too great a human and financial investment. Indeed, once departed, the workers in question must be replaced, to allow the levels of domestic agricultural activity to be maintained. The surplus of male labour, the lack of diversity regarding professional activities in the county, and the lack of agricultural yield are the reasons for which some of the menfolk leave for the cities. The principal activities of these unskilled workers are salvaging old furniture, demolishing old buildings, trade and catering. Men are considered to be the main source of income in the home (Chen 2006). Women stay at home with their children and are not considered to be part of the workforce as such, even though, during periods when their husbands are absent, the responsibility for working the fields falls to them. The absence of men results in a local shortage of agricultural labour and impoverishes family production. On the one hand, the income brought in by the exiled menfolk increases household resources, but on the other, the lack of male labour leads to decreased agricultural productivity and is accompanied by a loss of potential earnings.

Finally, drug trafficking (primarily heroin and opium) is also said thought to make up a significant part of Dongxiang's parallel economy. However, criminality in the region is currently little documented. I only know that a large portion of the local autonomous government's budget is put towards combating this trafficking; this part of the budget is greater than that allocated for the development of education. It should be noted that a significant number of men are currently incarcerated, leaving women and children to fend for themselves financially.

2.2.3 Social organisation of the group

Administrative organisation is hierarchically structured into four levels: the individual is part of a family (户 *hù*) that lives in a hamlet (村 *cūn*) located in a village (乡 *xiāng*) (Chen 2006). Dongxiang villages are generally organised in accordance with three criteria: family relationships, professional activities and religious affiliations.

Historically, social organisation has been related predominantly to professional activities since the Yuan dynasty (1271–1368). Today, only a few vestiges of this organisation remain in the county; thus, for example, the inhabitants of the village of Canfang 仓房 are, by tradition, felt makers (Chen 2006). From the Ming dynasty (1368–1644) onwards, given that society had become entirely agricultural following contact with the newly arrived Han Chinese[46], organisation based on blood ties began to replace that based on professional grouping. At the microsocial level, an individual (个人 *gèrén*) belongs to a family (家庭 *jiātíng*), which is included in a family circle (家伍 *jiāwǔ*), itself belonging to an extended family circle (大家伍 *dà jiāwǔ*), which is part of a clan (宗族 *zōngzú*). The organisation is patriarchal, based on the affiliation of brothers to their families. The highest authority is always represented by the oldest member of a clan (male or female, depending on the religious brotherhood). The third type of organisation is that of grouping by brotherhood. This system began around the 1770s, with the splintering of Islam into several schools in northwestern China, and the spread of Sufism. Today, there are five main orders comprising several dozen brotherhoods or sub-orders (Chen 2006). Four of the five main orders are Sufi: the Khafiyya (胡非林耶派 *Húfēilínyé pài*), the Jahriyya (哲赫林耶派 *Zhéhèlínyé pài*), the Qadriyya (嘎的林耶派 *Gādilínyé pài*) and the Kubriyya (库不林耶派*Kùbùlínyé pài*); the other is the fundamentalist order, the Ikhwan (伊赫瓦尼 *Yīhèwǎní*)[47]. Purists forbid marriage between members of different brotherhoods; readings of the Quran are not conducted together, and imams from different brotherhoods cannot act on one another's behalf in religious ceremonies. Today, religion is a systematic factor at all levels of social organisation; clan members may break away from their family and move to

46 See Zhao (2006).
47 See Israeli (2002).

another village in which the religious order is more appropriate for them, or they can even found their own brotherhood. This could be described as going 'back to basics'[48]; in other words, a return to the organisation that existed before the advent of the People's Republic of China in 1949, since which time Chinese rural areas have experienced a variety of agricultural reforms, moving from cooperative organisations (生产合作社 *shēngchǎn hézuòshè*), to people's communes (人民公社 *rénmín gōngshè*), to the final transformation of these systems into household responsibility groups (家庭联产承包责任制 *jiātíng liánchǎn chéngbāo zérèn zhì*). Social organisation was based on kinship relations, in which religious orders had been completely replaced by the political organisation system established by the government. Today, the political organisation is no longer the primary organisation in Dongxiang society, although it does still exist in the various local branches of the autonomous government.

At a macrosocial level, it is difficult to establish a class system, since the majority of the population is agricultural; average incomes do not really differ from one occupation to another, putting everyone at more or less the same economic level. Furthermore, most Dongxiang who achieve financial success relocate to larger cities, such as Linxia and Lanzhou. As Chen (2006) observes, this is particularly true for the rural areas in which the diversity of activities does not allow for clear boundaries to be drawn between the various sectors. For example, a peasant could simultaneously be an agricultural labourer when working in the fields, an independent entrepreneur when selling his sheep at the market, a labourer when helping to build houses, and so forth. However, I believe that social categories should be considered not in economic terms, but rather in terms of social prestige. It can be said that some activities are more highly regarded than others. Based on my observations in the field, I can generally establish different social levels linked to the sectors of activity in the county; these are valid for both urban and rural areas, and give us the following ranking, from least to most prestigious: (1) Farmer, (2) Teacher, (3) Shopkeeper, (4) Administrative officer and (5) Member of the clergy.

---

48 See Goldman (1986).

2.2.4 Education

2.2.4.1 Formal education

Since 1949, the establishment of schools and development of education in Dongxiang have experienced ups and downs, without being able to yield effective results. It was not until the 1980s that the number of schools began to increase and a genuine effort was made to create a literate population. However, the illiteracy rate among the Dongxiang has long been the highest in all of China; it stood at 89.31% of the population aged over 15 years old in 1982, and 63.29% in 2000 (Chen 2006). Furthermore, attitudes are still highly conservative, with the education of girls remaining rare until the early 2000s (see Table 2; Li 2007):

Table 2: Illiteracy rates among the Dongxiang

Year	Illiteracy rate (%)	Women (%)	Men (%)
1982	89.31	97.87	81.11
1990	88.00	96.90	79.70
2000	63.29	70.37	44.22

It should be noted, however, that it is difficult to interpret the figures in the table, given that the studies in question provide no information on the methodology used, nor any detail on the subject of the studies themselves. Indeed, it is very difficult to define the term "illiteracy" within the context of these studies, since they are based on the written production of Chinese characters, which raises questions inherent to mastery of the Chinese language (how many characters must one know in order to be considered literate? Can someone be considered literate if they only know how to read, without being able to produce written work? and so on). In 2011[49], there were 221 schools in Dongxiang County, including 190 primary schools, five middle schools and 3 secondary schools, staffed by 2,258 teachers and attended by 49,900 students.

Although there has been a marked improvement in the development of education in recent years, it nonetheless remains limited, since children's

49 *Statistical Bulletin on the Economic and Social Situation of Dongxiang Autonomous County*, Gansu Bureau of Statistics, 2011.

schooling generally ends at primary level, for both boys and girls. During the period from 2003 to 2008, in the five primary schools in the village of Beiling 北岭, the number of pupils fell by 20% per grade. Furthermore, the difference between mountainous and riverine areas, between the countryside and cities, is significant. In 2003, 67% of the county's girls were enrolled in school, but in the countryside (outside of towns), this figure was only 50%. The education of women is related to their social status; given that they are destined to serve their husband's family, their education does not represent a profitable investment. The problems that persist in education today are linked to the lack of correlation between the methods and content and the distinguishing linguistic, cultural and social characteristics of Dongxiang. Indeed, the content being taught is completely out of step with Dongxiang's social reality; this is largely due to the standardisation of school curricula in the People's Republic of China at a national level. Another major issue is that of geography; the lack of schools and teachers in mountainous areas means that 70.5% of pupils have to walk for more than an average of 30 minutes to get to school, and, of this figure, 31.5% have to walk for between one hour and more than two hours (Ma Yinian in Li 2007). This also means that a child cannot attend school until they are old enough to get there unsupervised[50]. As for older students attending secondary school, this necessarily involves enrolment at a school situated in a *zhen* or a town, and boarding school life; parents must therefore have the financial wherewithal to meet these expenses. Since an aim of education is to enable an individual to improve on the social status of their parents, in Dongxiang this means renouncing the social status of a farmer or unskilled worker. For young middle- or secondary-school leavers, two significant economic problems arise when looking for a job. First, the lack of diversity in professional activities and the unattractive remuneration of the jobs available (roughly equivalent to a farmer's income) in Dongxiang force them to leave the county. Second, the jobs market outside the county is so saturated that they are then obliged to return to places where the competition is less fierce, namely the environment they know best, that is, Dongxiang County. So their only option is to become an administrative officer, or to continue their studies and achieve

50 The only information available is from the 1990s (Wan 1991), which stated that, on average, Dongxiang children did not start school until the age of 9.

a level of education sufficient to make themselves competitive outside the county. In the first scenario, the position of basic state employee (干部 *gànbù*) has the disadvantage of attracting a very low salary (around 600 RMB[51] per month in 2005, Chen 2006), and in the second, there is the need for a financial investment that is impossible for families who, for the most part, are economically insecure. The level of education required to enable this social mobility is so high that many parents prefer not to send their children to school beyond the primary level, or even not to send them at all. The reform of minority languages undertaken in China in the 1950s did not at the time produce a written vehicle for the Dongxiang language, which still lacks a genuine system of writing that is understood across the community (Zhou 2003). As a result, formal education in state schools is traditionally delivered in Chinese, officially *Putonghua*, but in practice in Linxia (Hezhou hua) or by means of a linguistic compromise, depending on the teacher's level of education. Quality of teaching varies considerably, depending on whether the school is located in an urban or rural area, and the language in which education is delivered is one of the causes of academic underachievement. Indeed, until the early 2010s, teachers in schools located in market towns (*zhen*), with little or no command of *Putonghua*, would generally use Linxia or a mix of several Chinese dialects as their main medium of instruction. However, recent economic development and the opening up of Suonanba, thanks to new roads, have helped the town to raise its standard of living and wages, thereby attracting better-qualified teachers from northern China, who are more likely to use their own dialect than the actual standardised variety of *Putonghua*.

Several studies have been conducted on this subject (Su 1996; Li and Fu 2002; Zhang and Wang 2006), all of which show that the vast majority of children neither speak nor understand Chinese (of any dialect) when they start school. Consequently, they have great difficulty communicating, which leads to a lack of interest in lessons and, frequently, to academic underachievement. According to my observations in the field[52], primary schools'

---

51 In the mid-2000s, the salaries of administrative officers were halved, from 1300 to 600 TMB per month, in an effort to combat corruption by reorienting the interests of employees from their own finances to their work.

52 March 2010 and September 2014.

teachers alternate Dongxiang with *Putonghua* and Linxia during the first 3 or 4 years of primary school. So we have Dongxiang-speaking teachers always in charge of the earliest levels (often up to the third year), before handing over to teachers who are not speakers of the language. According to Ma Yinian et al. (2006, in Li et al. 2007), 48% of children understand no Chinese when they start school, be that either Linxia or *Putonghua*. Although the results obtained in Qi's study (2004) are only representative of the village of Laozhuang, they are, in my opinion, a fairly good reflection of the general situation in Dongxiang's isolated villages. In this village, 71% of the children (including those enrolled in school) understand little or no Chinese. In 2002, an experimental bilingual education programme was introduced for first- and second-year primary pupils in a school in Nalesi; a clear improvement (around 50%) in academic results was observed from the start of the programme (Chen 2006). Bilingual education thus appears to be one of the solutions that could help to resolve the issues related to the mother tongue of pupils. Another programme was established in 2008, and its scope extended to eighteen schools, but it ended in 2010[53] and has not been renewed. A similar bilingual education programme could also help to resolve identity issues because, as Zhang and Wang (2006) observe, some Dongxiang equate state schools with Han schools and consequently restrict access to school for fear that their children will be culturally assimilated. A writing system based on Arabic might also act as an incentive for the education of children. However, even though the basis for such a system has existed since the fifteenth century, for political reasons it has never been trialled.

In connection with the issues relating to parents' financial resources, in 2005 the state introduced the policy known as "Two Waivers and One Supplement" (两免一补 *liǎng miǎn yī bǔ*). This policy provides for the waiving of school fees and the costs of school equipment, and for the payment of a financial supplement for the accommodation costs related to schooling (boarding fees). It applies to both boys and girls from households experiencing financial difficulties. This policy has significantly reduced rates of absenteeism in schools, but more importantly, it has given girls the opportunity to receive an education on an equal footing with boys (Li 2007). However, although the figures show an increase in the enrolment rate in the first year,

53 To date, the results have not been made available.

discontinuation of studies between the second and fifth years remains at the same level.

The outcomes of this policy, however, are still largely constrained by social and religious factors, particularly owing to competition from informal, that is, religious education.

2.2.4.2 Informal education

Chinese researchers consider the Dongxiang to be an entirely Muslim community (Li 2006). Religious education is therefore a cultural and social necessity, as well as an economic one, for the vast majority of the population.

Generally speaking, children are sent to a mosque between the ages of 4 and 8 years, for a period of between a month and a year. This type of education has the advantage of being free, and the children are provided with meals. During this period, children learn to read the Arabic alphabet and the words that enable them to read the main passages of the Quran. Furthermore, education at the mosque is considerably more flexible than at a formal school. As the imam is usually a farmer himself, he follows the same working rhythm as the parents. As a result, holidays are scheduled to coincide with work in the fields, so children are at home when their parents most need their help. According to Zhang and Wang (2006), Arabic is often put on a pedestal when compared to Chinese; teaching it in state schools could solve the problem of academic underachievement, as parents would no longer be faced with the dilemma of having to choose between two types of education. They emphasise, however, that the most common criticism levelled at mosque education is that it is too focused on religion, to the detriment of other essential subjects, such as mathematics. From a practical perspective, for religious events involving the sacrifice of an animal, families are obliged to engage the services of an imam, whom they pay to say the prayers[54]. However, if someone in the family is competent to do this for them, the expense can be avoided. Furthermore, the future of children who have pursued religious studies is quite secure: they will become at least a *mala* 麻拉, a disciple who assists the imam at religious ceremonies, or better still,

54 Some Dongxiang insist that all animals eaten by them are slaughtered by an imam. However, the families we met only engaged the services of an imam for certain ceremonies.

an imam themselves; these are two well-paid professions compared to the other activities available in Dongxiang. The professional future of children who attend state schools is less certain.

The Dongxiang faithful do not all understand Arabic, which is why sermons in mosques are often delivered in Linxia and sometimes in Dongxiang, depending on the religious order and the geographic location of a mosque. Bao (2006) notes that the imam uses a type of unique language, the vocabulary of which is a mixture of Arabic, Persian and Chinese, with grammar following the word order of Linxia and other Chinese varieties. However, in isolated mountain villages, imams tend to routinely preach in Dongxiang, as the environment favours the exclusive use of this language. To the best of our knowledge, no document currently provides an account of the languages used in the mosques of Dongxiang, a subject that would merit a study in its own right.

And finally, in respect of women, once they are married, it is the men who are expected to provide their religious education. To this end, during the 1990s, some imams would record their speeches on audio cassette tape, in Linxia, for women. However, this practice appears to have become less widespread since the advent of the CD and the MP3.

2.2.5 Writing systems and graphic environment

Although it has no officially recognised writing system, there are in fact two notation systems for the Dongxiang language. The first of these, based on Arabic script, has existed since at least the fifteenth century, and the second, based on Chinese *Pinyin*, since 2001 (Ma and Chen 2001). Written vehicles do therefore exist, but their use is not widespread within the community. The first system is an ancient one, still used today in mosques, and the second is a recently created system, used only in a few primary schools, as part of the experimental bilingual education programme mentioned in Section 2.2.4.

Xiǎojīng 小经 (sometime written 消经) is a transcription system based on Arabic script, which itself has an alphabetical basis. The Dongxiang refer to it as *tǔhuà xiǎojīng* 土话小经 'little sacred book in the local language' (referring here to Dongxiang). This system is used to notate prayers and translate verses of the Quran, primarily for the purposes of religious education. Zhong (2007) adds that many people used this form of writing for correspondence, drafting contracts, recording important business deals and even for writing books. In the past, it was also used to record historical, literary and religious events. Use of this writing system began sometime in the fifteenth century; the Dongxiang consider it to be a transcription system specific to their language, referring to it as *tuhua orou*, or 'writing in the local language'. In actual fact, this notation system was borrowed from their Chinese-speaking neighbours, the Hui; the syllabic notation system of Chinese phonemes was retained, but was adapted and extended to encompass the specific phonological features of Dongxiang: of the alphabet's thirty-five letters, two are absent from the Arabic, Persian and Hui systems. The rest of the system is similar to the Hui's *xiaojing* system. Some researchers believe that *xiaojing* was invented by imams, for translating verses of the Quran and recording the names of the various religious organisations and brotherhoods, while others think that it was a transcription system invented for the purposes of social communication among a small section of the population[55]. Today, it is hardly ever used outside mosques, other than by a few old traders to record their inventories.

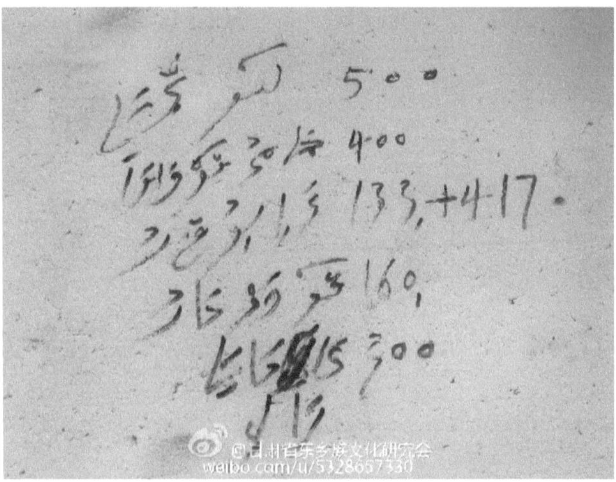

Photo 19: Dongxiang trader's records in *xiaojing* script[56].

55 See Ibrahim (2015).

56 Photo courtesy of Qiang Lihua, *Zhongguo Minzubao* (2015): <http://www.chinawriter.com.cn/mzwy/2015/2015-12-18/260979.htlm>.

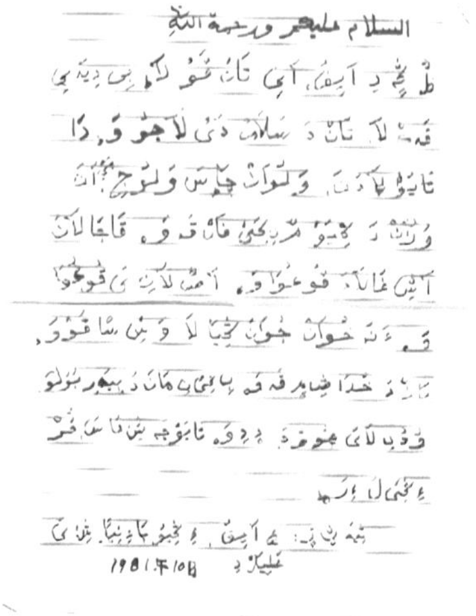

Photo 20: Personal correspondence in *xiaojing* script[57] dating from 1981.

Nie kewon nie usu tayi zhi durusen fugie gande anda bao wo

有个孩子掉到一口盛满水的大缸里了

ووژ ج بانژئن یئن ژا فوقو و

Uzhe zhi banjien yenjia fugu wo 眼看就要淹死

Pese de du kewosla ayi zhi holo wida wo

پسی دی دو کاوسلا ئي ایی ج حوتو ویدا و

其他孩子都吓跑了

Photo 21: Extract from a Dongxiang text written in *pinyin* and *xiaojing*, with its Chinese translation[58].

The *pinyin*-based transcription system is an alphabetical system, the use of which is limited to the first- and second-year syllabus of the experimental bilingual schools and a few sections of the local newspaper. It comprises

57 Photo courtesy of the Gansu Dongxiang Cultural Research Society (甘肃省东乡族文化研究会: https://weibo.com/u/5328657330).

58 Ibid.

fourty-four letter combinations, based on Chinese pronunciation, and enables the representation of Dongxiang phonemes. This is the system used in this work to transcribe the Dongxiang language (see Notes on the transcriptions).

The graphic environment within the borders of Dongxiang County consists mainly of signs and notices using Chinese characters. Commercial signage (businesses, shops and restaurants) routinely uses Chinese characters, usually indicating the name of the proprietor and the activity conducted on the premises. Sometimes, for restaurants, the word *halal* is written in Arabic next to the Chinese version 清真 (*qīngzhēn*). Walls are painted with government messages, in Chinese, of an educational or preventive nature. These messages relate to children's education, freedom of marriage, family planning, agrarian reform, etc.

Advertisements for telephone operators are also painted on both public and private walls. And finally, advertising posters, while still not found everywhere, are becoming increasingly common. Their main subject is health, and generally relate to hospitals (fertility treatment, heart problems, etc.). Schools and official institutions use external signage to display their key metrics (school enrolment figures, investment budgets, etc.). However, it must be acknowledged that these messages have little or no impact on the population since, as I mentioned earlier, approximately 65% of the population over the age of 15 years remains illiterate.

Photo 22: Official communication about birth control (main road from Maomao to Suonanba, March 2009)[59].

[59] Photo taken by the author in 2009.

In mosques and religious institutions, Arabic is the most widely used script, but some young *malas* prefer to use Chinese (Linxia and *Putonghua*) for making notes.

Recent urban development has resulted in a proliferation of schools, businesses and hospital facilities, creating a new economic dynamism in the heart of Suonanba, the capital of Dongxiang County. In parallel with the construction of these new buildings, messages using Chinese characters have become increasingly common. However, messages in Arabic are also on the increase, which is all the more surprising, as not only is there currently no policy in place to encourage the use of the Arabic alphabet, but, on the contrary, the use of Arabic is increasingly confined to the religious sphere. It would appear that, faced with globalisation and the growing ubiquity of Chinese characters, these Arabic messages are an assertion of identity[60].

Today, Suonanba is the only place with city-like characteristics, but even its outskirts melt into the ever-present surrounding countryside that dominates the rest of Dongxiang County.

2.2.6 Other socio-cultural aspects

2.2.6.1 Media and the internet

Dongxiang's first radio station appeared in 1952; in 1954 the cinema, now closed, opened its doors, and in 1974 the television station was established. There has also been print media, in *Putonghua*, since 1952. The television service broadcasts national channels, the Gansu channel and a local channel that mainly offers programmes in Chinese *Putonghua*, but no programmes in Dongxiang or Linxia are available on these channels. Today, however, many homes have satellite dishes that offer access to all the national and international channels authorised by the central government. Since 2007, the local newspaper has been publishing traditional stories in Dongxiang, in a special section that uses *pinyin*.

Furthermore, with the spread of new technologies in Dongxiang between 2010 and 2015, blogs and websites have proliferated. However, these are still written in Chinese, although some elements using Dongxiang and other local Chinese dialects can also be found. The aim of these sites is to disseminate

60 This situation has changed significantly since this study was conducted, with virtually no Arabic messages being visible in Suonanba today.

Dongxiang culture, not the language itself. They are very limited in number, and their content is closely controlled by the authorities.

In the late 2000s, access to the internet was extremely limited, with only one internet café in the whole county; this was reserved for individuals over the age of 18, in possession of a pre-registered identity card. Since the beginning of the 2010s, and particularly around 2013–2014, increased purchasing power and the introduction of newer technologies (such as 3G) in Dongxiang have enabled access to the internet from mobile phones, thereby democratising its use. However, the problem of illiteracy persists, and access to information remains limited.

2.2.6.2 Hua'er

A folk tradition, *Hua'er* 花儿 is a variety of song that is as likely to be heard in the mountains as in the fields, and is practised by various communities in Gansu, Qinghai and Ningxia. The Han, Hui, Salar, Yugur, Bonan, Monguor and Dongxiang communities all speak different languages, yet they all sing *Hua'er*. Little is known about its origin, but evidence of its use can be found in documents from the Ming and Qing dynasties (Zhao Zongfu 1988 in Zhong 2007) and was primarily sung by the Hui and Han communities. The structure of the songs can vary, but it is always regular, like that of a poem. There are several varieties, including *He Huang Hua'er* 河湟花儿, or the Hua'er of the region located between the Yellow River and the Huang River, straddling the provinces of Gansu and Qinghai, and of which Dongxiang is a part. Songs can be performed by an individual or in a group; they can also take the form of a vocal joust, in which the various participants respond to one another. *Hua'er* lyrics reflect the region's cultural and linguistic mix; most of the words are of Chinese origin, but there are also a few elements from minority languages, including words of Tibetan, Dongxiang, Mongguor, Mongolian, Salar, Arabic or Persian origin.

Zhong (2007: 84) gives the following example:

唱曲的尕妹妹甭呀兀列，小阿哥一 听是走哩

chang	*qu*	*di*	*ga*	*meimei*	*beng*	*ya*	*wulie*	*xiao*	*age*	*yi*
sing	song	GEN	little	little-sister	NEG	MP	NEG	little	elder.brother	one

ting	*shi*	*zou*	*li*
hear	cop	leave	fut

"The little girl can't help but sing, once a boy hears her, he'll come running."

In this sentence, *wulie* is borrowed from the Dongxiang *ulie*, meaning "not".

Since the 2000s, it has become customary for the Monguor of Qinghai to sing *Hua'er* in their own language; according to available documents, this was not previously the case, and seems to be a way of claiming their own ethnic identity, in much the same way as Tibetans do by singing in their language. The Dongxiang, emulating their Qinghai neighbours, have likewise begun singing in Dongxiang. However, the popularity of these songs in this language is not as great as that of songs in Chinese performed by a single popular singer, known to the majority of the Dongxiang community. *Hua'er* is never sung in both languages (bilingual Chinese-Dongxiang). This once-popular form of song no longer enjoys the success it once had, the younger generations preferring the trendy songs in Chinese *Putonghua* that are played in shops and public places, on local radio, television and on buses. The most popular 'ethnic' songs (民族歌 *mínzú gē*) are those of the Uyghurs and Tibetans, who perform in either their own language or in Chinese. As for the practice of *Hua'er* among young people, the only ones I encountered who still engage in this art form were the young residents of Hetan, a reputedly 'sinicised' village on the edges of the county.

2.2.6.3 Official institutions

The official institutions of Dongxiang Autonomous County's central government are mostly located in Suonanba. These include the seat of the autonomous government, the court, the hospital and the offices for taxation, business, police, budget and government coordination, etc. Other government institutions and offices can be found in the county's other towns and in the larger villages. The ethnic origin of members varies between offices and locations. Linxia is the primary vehicle of communication in the larger institutions (seat of the autonomous government, central police office), although Dongxiang is widely used between members of the same ethnic group. In the villages of the mountainous areas and the south, the latter is the main vehicle of communication. The choice of code is a personal choice for the speaker, although Dongxiang speakers mostly use Dongxiang in their language interactions with one another, and Linxia when speaking to people of other ethnic groups (Han and Hui). It appears evident that the situation is not straightforward, and that the language interactions between members of different communities within these institutions constitute a field worthy of a study in its own right. This is not the case for this study because, as we have already mentioned, the Dongxiang population is 96% rural; as the official institutions are concentrated in the towns, the employees of these eighty-five institutions total only around 7,500 individuals.

The Dongxiang Language and Its Linguistic Context

3.1 The Speakers of the Other Mongolic Languages of Gansu-Qinghai and Their Origin

According to the various researchers and classifications, the group of peripheral Mongolic languages in the Gansu-Qinghai region consists of five, six or seven languages.

Map 1: The Mongolic languages and the hybrid Chinese dialects of the Hexi Corridor.

The Bonan language is spoken by the Bonan (保安族 *Bǎo'ānzú*) ethnic group, and its speakers are concentrated in Jishishan Bonan, Dongxiang and Salar Autonomous County (积石山保安族东乡族撒拉族自治县 *Jīshíshān Bǎo'ānzú Dōngxiāngzú Sālāzú zìzhìxiàn*) in Gansu, and in the county of Tongren, situated in the Huangnan Tibetan Autonomous Prefecture (黄南藏族自治州同仁县 *Huángnán Zàngzú zìzhìzhōu Tóngrén xiàn*) in Qinghai.

The *Monguor* language, in reality, refers to three distinct, thought closely related varieties, Mangghuer, Mongghuor and Mongghul, which are spoken by a single officially recognised ethnic group: the Tu (土族 *tǔzú*) (Janhunen in Schram, 1957, reis. Stuart, 2006). Mongghul and Mongghuor are the varieties spoken in Huzhu Tu Autonomous County (互助土族自治县 *Hùzhù Tǔzú zìzhìxiàn*) in Qinghai, whereas the Mangghuer variety speakers of Mongguor are concentrated in the Minhe Hui and Tu Autonomous County (民和回族土族自治县 *Mínhé Huízú Tǔzú zìzhìxiàn*) in Gansu. Slater (2003) claims independent language status for Mangghuer, while Svantesson (2005) believes that, from a phonological point of view, the differences between Mongghul and Mangghuer do not justify this distinction and are instead the result of dialectal variations[61]. The Monguor languages spoken in the Huzhu region are often grouped into a single variety: Mongghul (Georg 2003). In our study, the term Mongghul will also be used to refer to the two varieties spoken in Huzhu.

Eastern Yugur[62] (or Shira Yugur) is spoken by the Yugurs (裕固族 *Yùgùzú*), also known as the Yellow Yugurs, who are mainly found in the Sunan Yugur Autonomous County (肃南裕固族自治县 *Sùnán Yùgùzú zìzhìxiàn*).

Finally, the Dongxiang language is spoken by the Dongxiang people, mainly in Dongxiang Autonomous County (东乡族自治县 *Dōngxiāngzú zìzhìxiàn*) and Jishishan Bonan, Dongxiang and Salar Autonomous County in Gansu (see Map 1), but also in Yining County (伊宁县 *Yīníng xiàn*) and Huocheng County (霍城县 *Huòchéngxiàn*), located in Yili Kazakh Autonomous Prefecture (伊犁哈萨克自治州 *Yīlí Hāsàkè zìzhìzhōu*) in Xinjiang[63].

---

61 For more on the proximity between the Monguor languages, see Gruntov & Mazo (2019).

62 The Yugur ethnic group recognised by the People's Republic of China includes two groups of speakers who speak two distinct languages: Eastern Yugur, a Mongolic language and Western Yugur, a Turkic language.

63 Some Dongxiang settled in Xinjiang in the 1950s. There are about 45,000 individuals there.

To these languages, Sechenchogt (1999), Delige'erma and Bo (2006) and Lattimore (in Schram 2006) added Kangjia (康家语 *Kāngjiā yǔ*), a language spoken by a number of Hui in Kangyang Township, situated in Jianzha County (尖扎县康杨镇 *Jiānzhā xiàn Kāngyáng zhèn*) in Qinghai. Kangjia's status as an isolated Mongolic language remains poorly established, however, and although several descriptions of the language exist (Xi 1995; Sechenchogt 1999), most comparative studies of this region accord it only a mention.

If we examine the common characteristics and the linguistic differences (see Section 3.2) found in these languages, we can divide their formation period into two phases: first, a formation phase from a linguistic substrate originating in Middle Mongolian or Turkic languages, followed by a second phase during which these languages have been influenced by a local superstrate, including various varieties of Chinese and Tibetan.

Indeed, a certain number of linguistic elements can be found in these peripheral languages that researchers (Field 1997; Buhe 1986; Nugteren 2011; Bao 2006) have identified as archaisms inherited from Middle Mongolian, such as the conservation of certain phonemes, a proportion of the vocabulary (including grammatical words), and certain syntactic structures. This demonstrates their direct connection with Middle Mongolian and their common heritage. There is also commonality between the parts of their vocabulary of Turkic origin, a characteristic absent in non-peripheral Mongolic languages (Field 1997). Chen (2006) correlates these linguistic elements with historical information and asserts that these populations came predominantly from Central Asia, deported together during the same period, that of the conquest of Xi Xia mentioned above; it is thought that this is how they came to be grouped together in the regions of Hexi 河西 and Hehuang 河湟[64]. All these groups speaking different Mongolic languages are therefore believed to have the same origin. After the conquest of Xi Xia, they are thought to have stayed in situ and mixed with the local populations, who spoke various Chinese and Tibetan languages and varieties thereof.

64 He 河 for Huanghe 黄河 the 'Yellow River' and Huang 湟 for Huangshui 湟水, a tributary of the Yellow River. This region is also known as the Hexi Corridor or the Gansu Corridor, terms that refer to one of the most important Silk Roads in history, connecting Northern China to the Tarim Basin and Central Asia.

Indeed, it is possible that these people may have originally spoken various Turkic languages, before adopting the language of their leaders, Mongolian, the dominant lingua franca of that time. There would thus have been a language shift. Field (1991) adds that for the Dongxiang language specifically, this would essentially have been a Mongol-Turkic pidgin or creole. According to him, certain linguistic characteristics of Dongxiang, primarily the absence of vowel harmony and of long vowels (characteristics that are, incidentally, shared by several other peripheral Mongolic languages), are more likely to have been the result of imperfect learning[65] of Middle Mongolian by Dongxiang speakers than of the direct influence of Linxia, the neighbouring Chinese dialect. In other words, the language transfers from Turkic language(s) (the source language(s)) to Middle Mongolian (the target language) resulted in interferences. This phenomenon, known as substrate interference, appears when the group transferring its language(s) is socio-politically subordinate to the other group of speakers (Thomason 2001). Indeed, socio-historical information suggests that this could very well have been the case for Dongxiang. Furthermore, imperfect learning and its process include elements that vary in accordance with the level of integration of the transferring linguistic community into the new linguistic community. Initially, the learners transfer elements from the source language to the target language, thereby creating a modified target language. In the case of the Dongxiang language, these elements are evidenced by the vocabulary of Turkic origin. Subsequently, errors resulting from learners' failure to learn certain elements of the source language contribute to the establishment of the modified target language. If the transferring group is not integrated into the target-language linguistic community, then its members remain a separate ethnic or national entity, and the modified target language then becomes the final version of the target language for this particular linguistic community. If the transferring group is integrated into the target-language linguistic community, the modified target language and the target language may blend, thereby creating a second modified target language which then becomes the shared language of the whole linguistic community (Thomason 2001). In the case of the Dongxiang language, the linguistic group of the transferring community is not thought to have been integrated into the linguistic community of the target language,

65 See Section 3.2.

and thus established its own ethnic group, the Dongxiang. Today's Muslim populations (the Dongxiang and the Gansu Bonan) are therefore believed to be composed essentially of Huihui Semu and of Mongols converted to Islam[66]. The Buddhist groups (the Monguor, the Qinghai Bonan and the Yugur) were themselves probably converted through contact with Tibetans. The formation of the various groups and the evolution of their languages is thus believed to have been closely linked to their religions.

However, from a linguistic point of view, imperfect learning and its resulting interferences are often caused by the absence of a characteristic in the source language, making its reproduction in the target language impossible. Vowel harmony and long vowels, characteristics absent from certain peripheral Mongolic languages, are present in Old Turkic (Erdal 2004) and are shared by all Turkic languages (Poppe 1955a). It therefore seems difficult to assert, at least due to the absence of these two characteristics in the Dongxiang language, that this is the result of imperfect learning.

The ethnic representations of these groups should enable their common origin to be established. However, the Minhe Monguor people refer to themselves using the term Mangghul, which, according to them, indicates their kinship with their Mongol ancestors (Slater 2003). The term *mongguor* has the same origin, but the transformation of the final consonant **l* > **r* is the result of a phonetic evolution due to the influence of Tibetan. Also, even if the hypothesis of the Sarta or even Turkic origin of the Dongxiang seems well-founded, it is much less so regarding the Mongguors. One can hypothesise that these two groups have different origins (Mongol for the Monguor people, *sarta* and Turkic for the Dongxiang), or that they are of the same origin but claim a different one in accordance with their religious affiliations.

According to the available historical information, the second transformation phase of these languages, under the influence of external linguistic groups, appears to have begun at the start of the Ming dynasty (1369–1664). Indeed, it was specifically during the reign of the Hongwu Emperor (1368–1398) that a significant immigration movement of the Han populations began, primarily from the eastern part of the empire[67].

66 We know, for example, that the Prince of Anxi 安西, Ananda (?–1307), grandson of Kublai Khan, converted thousands of his troops to Islam (Dunnell 2014).

67 See Zhao (2006).

This resulted in populations originating in the Blue River and Huai regions, and in the provinces of Hunan, Sichuan, Shanxi, Shaanxi and Gansu, relocating to the Hehuang region. Some of this migration was voluntary, but much was due to the forced relocation of farmers and convicts[68]. It would therefore be due to the influence of the new immigrant populations that a proportion of Muslims adopted Chinese and that, among other varieties, Hezhou (today's Linxia) came to be formed. According to Schram (2006: 114), Sinophone Muslims were of Turkic origin, but, through contact with the Chinese, they adopted the language and a number of Chinese customs. From this period onwards, the cultural and linguistic influence of the Han Chinese continued to grow in this region. While some groups of speakers adopted the language of the dominant newcomers, others, more isolated, retained their own language; the Dongxiang are believed to be among the latter. In the case of the Chinese dialect of Linxia (Hezhou hua), certain characteristics, such as the dominant SOV syntactic order, the use of case markers, and the presence of words of Mongol origin, are thought to be either the residue of the Mongol substrate or the result of intensive contacts with other Altaic languages such as Dongxiang.

This is also believed to be the way in which the various Mongolic languages of the region were formed: independently, with each acquiring specific linguistic characteristics. Through contact with other surrounding languages, these Mongolic languages have, in turn, developed dialects; from Monguor, at least the three varieties already mentioned: Mangghuer, Mangghul and Mongghuor and from Bonan, the Jishishan and Tongren varieties, the latter including the two sub-varieties, gNan Thog and Xiazhuang[69]. Intelligibility between these dialects, spread along the Gansu-Qinghai border area, is not always possible, at least for Monguor (Dede 2007). Conversely, with regard to Bonan, Wu Hugjiltu (2003) attests that mutual intelligibility between these two groups, despite them no longer being in regular contact, is reported (by speakers) to still exist, should communication between them be necessary. Dongxiang, whose speakers have largely remained concentrated in

68 Chen (2006: 49).

69 We can observe that the comparative studies conducted in China on the Mongolic languages (Delige'erma 2006; Zhong 2007; Sun 1987) almost never consider the various language varieties.

their present area, has developed no known dialect or specific variety[70]. The Dongxiang of Xingjiang have probably developed a different variety of their language, but studies of this issue currently remain limited[71].

3.2 The Dongxiang Language and the Mongolic Languages of Gansu-Qinghai

The Mongolic languages of Gansu-Qinghai have retained certain characteristics specific to Mongolic languages, but have lost others through the influence of languages belonging to other language families. These same external influences encouraged the preservation of certain specific features of Middle Mongolian, but these have now completely disappeared in Modern Mongolian. As a result, these languages form a separate group within the family of Mongolic languages and are referred to as "peripheral", owing to their geographical location in relation to other Mongolic languages and their specific linguistic characteristics.

The influence of exogenous factors on these languages has been so profound that it is sometimes difficult to establish precisely to what extent a feature is a common genetic inheritance from a common 'source language' that predates the formation of the Mongolic languages as they are currently distributed. As Slater (2003) points out, it is perfectly possible for a feature to be borrowed from a source language and then diffused across other Mongolic languages through contact between them. This is true, for example, for a phonetic characteristic representative of this group: the initial *h*. Indeed, Nugteren (2011) shows that, in these languages, this phoneme at the beginning of words of Mongolic origin is more often than not a legacy of Middle Mongolian, and that it has disappeared in Modern Mongolian. However, the initial *h* found in Middle Mongolian does not always correspond to those found in the Mongolic languages of Gansu-Qinghai. Some initial '*h*'s may have initially developed in Mongguor, through an internal mechanism, and then spread into the vocabularies of other Mongolic languages in the region (Slater 2003; Svantesson 2005).

70 There are variations of accent between the various Dongxiang villages, but these differences are not sufficient to establish proof of obvious varieties.

71 See Qian (2010) and Gui (2010) for partial descriptions.

According to the studies of these languages, at the lexical level, the proportion of vocabulary of Mongolic origin ranges from 39% to 77%. Vocabulary of Chinese origin is of varying influence, depending on the language and dialect, but nevertheless represents a significant source of borrowings in all of the languages (Janhunen, 2003), whereas borrowings from Tibetan are found predominantly in the languages spoken in the Qinghai region. As for Bonan, figures for borrowed vocabulary differ widely between studies (Chen 2006; De and Bo 2006; Rybatzki 2003), which do not always take into account the dialectal differences of this language.

Shira Yugur and Mongguor are the languages with the highest percentage of vocabulary of Mongolic origin (Table 3).

Table 3: Vocabulary of the Mongolic languages of Gansu-Qinghai[72]

Origin of vocabulary	Mongolic	Tibetan	Chinese
Bonan (Gansu)	43%	17%	40%
Bonan (Qinghai)	44%	42%	9%
Mangghuer	39%	?	?
Mongghuor/Mongghul	72%	12%	13%
Dongxiang	56%	< 1%	42%
Shira Yugur	77%	3%	5.4%

At the phonological level, Janhunen (2006) believes that the Mongolic languages of the Gansu-Qinghai region, much like the Turkic languages, have lost most of their original phonological characteristics. Their phonetic systems have been completely replaced by those of either Bodic or Sinitic languages, depending on the influence to which they were exposed. Mangghuer and Dongxiang thus adopted the Sinitic system, while Mongghul, Shira Yugur and Bonan[73] adopted the Bodic system. Vowel harmony, which has been partially retained in Shira Yugur, has been all but eliminated in Mangghuer and Mongghuor, and is completely absent in Bonan and Dongxiang (De and Bo 2006). Opposition between long and short vowels is present in all of the languages, except for Dongxiang, Mangghuer and Gansu (Jishishan) Bonan (Bao 2006).

72 Data compiled from the following studies: Chen (1987), Buhe (1986), Delige'erma and Bo (2006), Slater (2003), Field (1991), Fried (2010), Georg (2003) and Wu (2003).

73 It is likely that the phonetic system of Gansu Bonan was not completely replaced and was also influenced by Chinese.

The stress on the final syllable of words, common to all these languages, is a feature specific to the Mongolic languages of Gansu-Qinghai, and is not found in any other language of the Mongolic family. This point causes differences of opinion among researchers; Slater (2003) believes that it is an innovation, insofar as all the Mongolic languages of Gansu-Qinghai may have originally placed stress on initial syllables, but subsequently, and for reasons that he does not define, adopted stress on final syllables. Indeed, it is possible that under the influence of a Turkic language, such as Western Yugur (西部裕固语 *xībù yùgù yǔ*), this characteristic may have spread initially to Shira Yugur (东部裕固语 *dōngbù yùgù yǔ*), the closest neighbouring language, and then to all the surrounding Mongolic languages. Field (1997), on the other hand, believes that it is a retention; according to him, the presence of stress on the final syllables is an inherited feature, indicating a substratum of Turkic origin. Rybatzki (2003) attempts a classification based on thirty-two phonological and forty-one morphosyntactic features likely to be shared by the world's various Mongolic languages[74]. He concludes that Dongxiang is as close to Gansu Bonan as it is to Mangghuer, and that the similarities between Mongghul and Bonan (thirty-four shared features) and those between Mangghuer and Dongxiang (thirty-three shared features) are due to the parallel impact of the influence of a non-Mongolic language, namely Tibetan in the case of Mongghul and Bonan, and Chinese in the case of Mangghuer and Dongxiang.

Shira Yugur acts as a bridge between the two groups, the northern and the Gansu-Qinghai, since it shares similarities with Oirat, a Mongolian dialect of the western group, and with the languages of Gansu-Qinghai (Nugteren 2003). In fact, the Deed Mongols, who live in Subei Mongol Autonomous County (肃北蒙古族自治县 *Sùběi Měnggǔzú zìzhìxiàn*) in Gansu and are neighbours of the Yugurs, speak a variety of Oirat; it is therefore possible that contact between the two populations influenced Shira Yugur and led to the retention and development of certain features common to other Mongolic languages.

Tables 4 and 5 provide a summary of the main phonological, morphological and syntactic[75] features shared by, or inherent to, at least one Gansu-Qinghai Mongolic language:

---

74 Dagur, Khamnigan, Buryat, Khalkha, Ordos, Oirat, Moghol, Shira Yugur, Mongghul, Mangghuer, Bonan and Dongxiang.

75 The features selected here were chosen from the seventy-four features identified by Rybatzki (2003: 364–384).

Table 4: Phonological characteristics of the Mongolic languages of Gansu-Qinghai

Language Feature	Mongghul	Mangghuer	Bonan (Gansu)	Bonan (Qinghai)	Dongxiang	Shira Yugur	Modern Mongolian
Phonetic System	Tibetan	Chinese	Chinese	Tibetan	Chinese	Tibetan	Mongolian
Short vowels	5	5	6	6	6	8	11
Long vowels	+	-	-	+	-	+	+
Vowel harmony	traces	traces	-	-	-	partial	+
Labial harmony	-	-	-	-	-	-	+
Neutralisation **ö* **ü* > (**o*) (**u*)	+	+	+	+	+	-	-
MM distinction Of **k* **g* vs **q* **gh*	-	-	-	-	+	-	-
MM initial **h-*	+	+	+	+	+	+	-
Retention of **x*	+	+	+	+	+	+	-
Development of **ɕ* and **ʂ*	+	+	+	?	+	-	-
Stress	final	final	final	final	final	final	initial
Initial consonant cluster	+	-	+	+	-	+	-
Sonant assimilation	partial	partial	partial	partial	partial	partial	full
Palatalisation of **t* and **d*	-	-	-	-	+	-	-

Table 5: Morphosyntactical characteristics of the Mongolic languages of Gansu-Qinghai

Language Feature	Mongghul	Mangghuer	Bonan Gansu	Bonan Qinghai	Dongxiang	Shira Yugur	Modern Mongolian
*_n_ voiceless in the nominative	+	+	- (lexicalised)	- (lexicalised)	- (lexicalised)	+	-
Sg marker	+	+	+	+	-	-	-
Genitive/accusative convergence	+	+	+	+	+	+	-
Accusative/dative convergence	+ (partial)	+ (partial)	+ (partial)	+ (partial)	-	-	-
Comitative/instrumental convergence	+	+	+	+	+	+	-
Classifiers	-	+	-	-	+	-	-
Reflexive pronoun *_ejen_	+	+	+	+	+	+	- (*öxen)
Demonstrative. *_ene_	+	+	+	+	+	+	- (*üün)
Possessive suffix	-	-	-	-	+	+	+
Narrative *_-m_	+	-	+	+	-	-	-
Resultative *_-ji- / jixAi_	+	+	+	+	-	-	+
Concession converb -_senu_	-	-	-	-	+	-	-
Perfective *_–san_	+	+	+	+	+	-	+
Habitative *_-dag_	-	-	-	-	-	+	+
Non-finite converb *_gsA/xAr_	+	+	+	+	-	-	+
Final GRD *_-la_	+	+	+	+	+	+	-
Consecutive GRD -Ø	+	+	+	+	+	+	-
Perfective GRD *_-xad_	-	-	-	-	-	+	+
Borrowed medial copula *_shi_	-	+	+	-	+	-	-
Category of perspective	+	+	+	+	-	-	-
MM negations *ülü	+	+	+	+	+	+	-

Dongxiang shares most of the retentions from Middle Mongolian with all of the region's other Mongolic languages, along with the innovations preserved or developed subsequently. It is distinguishable from the other peripheral languages through two phonological and two morphological characteristics. It is the only language to have preserved the distinction between **k *g* et **q *gh*, which is a retention from Middle Mongolian. Furthermore, through the influence of Linxia, the phonemes **t* and **d* have been systematically palatalised. From a morphological perspective, even though all the region's Mongolic languages have developed a concession converb, it is the only one to have done so using the form **-senu*. However, there is no non-finite converb in Dongxiang, whereas this feature is present in all other languages in the region. All other characteristics are shared with at least one of the region's other Mongolic languages.

The emergence of certain similar features in different languages is probably due to the influence of Chinese on each of them; however, it is likely that these features have developed independently of one another. For example, this is certainly the case for the use of the borrowed medial copula *shi* in Mangghuer, Gansu Bonan and Dongxiang, and for the partial lexicalisation of the so-called voiceless, or unstable **-n* in Dongxiang and Gansu Bonan. The other common features (be they retentions, innovations or eliminations) are due to the influence of other, non-Mongolic languages.

From all these observations, the conclusion emerges that the Mongolic languages of Gansu-Qinghai should be classified in accordance with the nature of the superstratum that influenced them, taking particular account of their geographical distribution: the eastern Mongolic languages (Mongghuor and Qinghai Bonan), located mainly in Qinghai, have been heavily influenced by Tibetan; those in the west (Gansu Bonan and Dongxiang), located in Gansu and northern Qinghai, have themselves been influenced by Chinese, and those in the north (Eastern Yugur and Oirat), by Turkic. Mangghuer appears to have been more heavily influenced by Chinese than Mongghuor, and thus plays a buffer role within its group. Dongxiang has no particular status within the Gansu-Qinghai group. It can be defined as (1) the language that has adopted the fewest features from Tibetan and (2) one of the languages that has adopted the most features from Chinese.

3.3 The Region's 'Hybrid' Chinese Languages and Linxia

In addition to the Mongolic languages, this area is also home to speakers of Tibeto-Burman (Amdo Tibetan), Turkic (Salar and Western Yugur) and a number of Sinitic languages, which researchers include in the Gansu-Qinghai Sprachbund. The latter are the Wutun 五屯, Gangou 甘沟, Linxia 临夏 and Tangwang 唐汪 varieties, all of which Chinese linguists classify as belonging to the Northwest Chinese dialectal subgroup (西北方言 *Xīběi fāngyán*) (Luo 2004), but which, owing to their characterising linguistic features, could merit the status of independent languages.

Influenced by the various languages of this region, they have in fact developed certain original features which, although rarely observed in other Sinitic languages, are common to all Mongolic and Turkic languages. These include the SOV syntactic order and the inflectional morphology found in all Chinese varieties of the region, which are features common to the Mongolic and Turkic languages from which they have, in all probability, been borrowed (Dwyer 1992; Lee-Smith 1996).

Studies by Peyraube (2015) and Xu (2015a) catalogue the case markers in these languages, thereby demonstrating that at least three forms of case marker are similar and are shared by all varieties of Chinese. The presence of these linguistic features can be explained by two sociolinguistic phenomena: *relexification* (Muysken 1981) and *regrammaticalisation* (DeGraff 2002).

Relexification involves the replacement of the lexicon of a language, L1, by that of another, L2, without changing the syntax and morphology of the substratum (L1).

On the basis of available historical evidence, and if we accept that the speakers had adopted Mongolian as their vehicular language under the rule of Genghis Khan in the fourteenth century, they may have succeeded in retaining some features of their source language (Middle Mongolian) during the process of language transfer to the target language (Chinese). In other words, the speakers may have sought a linguistic compromise between the two languages, whereby the syntactic structure of their L1 (Middle Mongolian) was retained, while Chinese (L2) became the main source of vocabulary. These features would thus constitute linguistic interferences, the presence of these grammatical elements reflecting the influence of a substratum of Mongolic (or Turkic or both) origin, and be the result of "imperfect learning". The Han Chinese, thereafter arriving in the region in greater numbers, would have mixed with the local populations already speaking this variety, later adopting it as their mother tongue and developing dialects that were, in turn, influenced by the other surrounding languages, thereby resulting in the establishment of the various varieties of Chinese encountered in this region.

The presence of these distinctive Chinese dialects can also be explained by the exogenous influence of the Mongolic languages. Chinese speakers are thought to have borrowed just a small part of the vocabulary of Mongolic origin, but a significant number of Mongolic syntactic elements: that is, there was an occurrence of the phenomenon of regrammaticalisation. This involves the replacement of syntax and morphology with a superstrate language (L2), while the lexical roots of the source language (L1) are retained. In other words, as a result of the influence of the Mongolic and/or Turkic languages (L2) already spoken in the Gansu region, immigrant speakers arriving in the region modified the varieties of Chinese they spoke (L1), borrowing morphosyntactical elements yet retaining most of their original Chinese lexicon.

To recap, in the case of relexification, the source language (L1) would have been a Mongolic language (the substratum) that was the subject of a language transfer to the Chinese language (L2), with imperfect learning among the community of speakers. As for regrammaticalisation, the Chinese dialects would have been the substratum, influenced by the syntax of the surrounding Mongolic languages (the superstratum) and resulting in significant syntactical modification.

For either of these phenomena, the process has led to the emergence of new linguistic varieties that are specific to the socio-historical context in which these languages were formed. According to Wittmann (1993), both relexification and regrammaticalisation are linked to the social context of language formation, which can only be identified retrospectively. Regrammaticalisation occurs when a vehicular language, or *lingua franca*, becomes universally accessible to a newly formed population of diverse origin, whereas relexification does not necessarily require language transfer, but results from endogamous social practices that are characteristic of the formation of an independent collective identity. However, available historical information provides us with no indication of exactly when these Chinese languages were formed, nor of their particular social context. Furthermore, it is not possible to identify the languages in question with any degree of accuracy. Many questions remain unresolved. Was the substratum, source language or L1, the Middle Mongolian that we see in written sources? Could it have been a dialect? A modified version of Middle Mongolian? Or a Turco-Mongolic pidgin spoken by people of diverse origin who had been speakers of various languages? Was the Mongolian substratum an established, stabilised language, or a mixed language? And was the superstratum, target language or L2, a uniform variety of a Chinese dialect from another region, or was it a linguistic compromise, a mix of several varieties spoken by people from different regions?

Moreover, it is impossible to determine whether the process by which these Sinitic languages were formed was the same for all Mongolic languages, or whether they evolved independently, but in a context involving contact between similar languages.

Of all these varieties, the Hezhou dialect is the most sociolinguistically significant, as it is considered to be the *lingua franca* of the entire region. Indeed, it is not only the mother tongue of the Hui and Han people living in the Linxia Hui Autonomous Prefecture, but also the second language of those in Jishishan Bonan, Dongxiang and Salar Autonomous County and in Xunhua Salar Autonomous County (Lee-Smith 1996). The exact number of speakers has not been established but, by our estimates, there are around two million of them.

Dongxiang County is in direct contact with two particular varieties of the Hezhou dialect: Tangwang, which is spoken in the village of Tangwang, on the outskirts of the County, and Linxia, which is spoken in the city of Linxia, approximately 25 km from Suonanba. These two varieties are similar, and have been in intense contact with the Dongxiang language owing to their geographical proximity. The genesis of these two varieties, and their development processes, have yet to be explained.

Most Dongxiang speak fluent Linxia, or at least a variety that is very close to it[76]. Dongxiang has been chiefly influenced by this language, and has borrowed extensive lexical elements from it[77]. Works on Linxia were

---

76 See Min (2018) for a description of the variety of Chinese spoken in Dongxiang.

77 See Chapter 5.

first published in the 80s (Ma 1984; Ma 1988), and have continued to appear quite regularly since then (Liu et al. 1996; Luo 2004; Guo 2006; Min 2016), while those on Tangwang have only appeared recently. Djamouri (2015), Xu (2015b) and Cao et al. (2015) analysed some of the syntactic elements borrowed by Tangwang from Mongolic and Turkic languages, but were not able to determine a single source for this borrowing.

Linxia is considered by some researchers to be a creole (see Lee-Smith 1996), but I think it would be more accurate to call it a 'hybrid language', that is 'a language that borrows certain features from two or more languages' (Kortas 2009), as the term 'creole' applies to very specific sociolinguistic contexts. Arends, Myusken & Smith (1995) considered that creoles share the following characteristics: (1) they form part of a group of languages that are typologically similar in many ways; (2) they are simpler than their source languages; (3) they have a high degree of syntactic diversity and (4) they have a high degree of variation. This does not appear to be the case with the above-mentioned Chinese varieties, Linxia included, which are both semantically and syntactically complex. Moreover, many linguists admit that it is impossible to identify common linguistic traits for creole languages that are not also shared with isolating languages (Thomasson 1997; Mufwene 1998).

Linxia is characterised phonologically by only three tones (as compared to the four tones of most north-western Mandarin dialects) and at least three phonemes borrowed from Tibetan (Liu et al. 1996). Its lexicon, mostly of Chinese origin, has retained some words and expressions from ancient Chinese, and borrowed others from the surrounding Mongolic and Turkic languages. As mentioned above, the syntactic elements clearly reflect the influence of Altaic languages. Indeed, the partial SOV order (as opposed to the SVO order of most north-western Chinese dialects) and the inflectional morphology, as evidenced by the presence of cases, nominal plural markers, (causative) diatheses and opposition between finite and non-finite aspects (participles and converbs), are characteristics of the neighbouring Mongolic and Turkic languages. Thus, from a syntactic perspective, Linxia is closer to Dongxiang than to the other Mandarin dialects of the northwest.

In this work, therefore, I will make a distinction between the north-western Mandarin dialects, *putonghua* and Linxia when referring to Chinese. The term "north-western Mandarin dialects" covers the varieties of Chinese, including *zhongyuan guanhua* (中原官话) and *lanying guanhua* (兰银官话),

that are spoken in Gansu and Qinghai, which differ from both the standard language, *putonghua*, and the 'hybrid' dialects of Gansu-Qinghai mentioned above. Hence, it pertains to all the varieties of Chinese spoken in the Gansu-Qinghai region, other than the 'hybrid' varieties. This simplified designation allows room for a much more complex reality, without dismissing the challenges that the genealogy and precise categorisation of Chinese dialects still pose to this day.

The Dongxiang Linguistic Community

4.1 Identity Representations: The Perception of Self and Other

Prior to the advent of the PRC in 1949, the Dongxiang were grouped together with, and considered themselves part of, the Hui, especially those from Linxia, their nearest neighbours. Under Qing (1644–1911) rule and until the early days of the Republic of China (1911), populations were classified into five distinct categories: Mongol, Manchu, Tibetan, Hui and Han. The Hui category referred to a religious identity, with no genetic or linguistic connotations. Indeed, the Hui have no language of their own, and generally speak the Chinese dialect local to the region in which they are established. The assimilation of the Dongxiang into this group thus seemed natural, since there were no cultural barriers preventing this from occurring. That is how their essentially Muslim identity, a combination of culture and religion, was created.

Linguistically, as the Dongxiang language is related to that of the Mongols (see Section 3.1), they were also able to integrate with the latter in the pre-communist (1949) era. They thus called themselves *Dongxiang-Hui* (东乡回) 'The Hui of the eastern village', *Dongxiang-Menggu* (东乡蒙古) 'The Mongols of the eastern village', *Menggu-Hui* (蒙古回) 'The Hui-Mongols' or even *Dongxiang-Turen* (东乡土人) 'The locals of the eastern village'; each of these names referring to their territory, religion and/or language. The name Dongxiang-Turen is also related to the language spoken by the Dongxiang, since they themselves refer to it as 'tuhua' (from the Chinese *tǔ huà* 土话)

Lit.: 'the local language[78]'. Turen refers to nothing other than 'local people', so Dongxiang-Turen literally means 'the local people of Dongxiang' or 'the population living in Dongxiang'.

The Dongxiang identity, as defined by other communities, was therefore based on religious, linguistic and territorial elements.

After 1949, the communists, who had recently risen to power, implemented the principles of Stalinist theory on minorities[79]. As a result, the Soviet model was applied almost systematically to establish the status of national minorities (Ma 2004) and a campaign to identify nationalities was carried out throughout China. The eligibility criteria were based on a number of points, including the historical formation of a community, its stability, a common language, a common territory and a shared culture (Zhou 2003). These criteria were not applied equally to all communities, resulting in the creation of some groups that were basically indistinguishable from one another, while leaving others without minority status, despite claiming it. This campaign led to the establishment of fifty-six nationalities (民族 *mínzú*), of which fifty-five were minority ethnic groups (少数民族 *shǎoshù mínzú*). The situation of the Dongxiang matched these linguistic, territorial and cultural criteria perfectly; they were therefore accorded national minority status, with the Chinese name *dōngxiāng zú* (东乡族), 'Dongxiang nationality', and granted the right to form their own local autonomous government.

The Hui, despite some issues of definition, obtained the same status on the basis of their common religion. So it was only from this point that the Hui and Dongxiang were considered to be two distinct groups, the languages that they spoke having become a conscious criterion of ethnic differentiation.

The Dongxiang also used, and continue to use, the term Santa to refer to their own group and all the other Muslim groups[80]. Hence, the Xinjiang Uyghurs are, even today, considered to be Santa by the Dongxiang people. In the Dongxiang language, there is even the term 'Santa oron', meaning

---

78 This name has been interpreted by some researchers as an abbreviation of "Turk" (土尔其) *tǔ ěr qí* or *Tǔzú* (土族), the Chinese name for the Monguor. In any case, I believe the term *tuhua* has no relationship with these two words, as many other communities also refer to the local language with this name (e.g., Mauritius' Chinese community refers to the local creole language as *tuhua*).

79 See Zhou (2003).

80 See Section 2.1.2.

'Santa countries' or 'Muslim countries', which is used to refer to all countries, regions and territories in which there are Muslims (Chen 2007). Santa, therefore, does not describe a specific ethnic group, and is the equivalent of the term Hui as it was used in pre-PRC times.

This is why the Dongxiang make no clear distinction between Hui and Santa, since for them, the word 'Santa' equates to the word 'Hui' in their own language. They are, therefore, still assimilated with the Hui from a cultural and religious perspective.

Grossberg (1993) says that 'the identity of any term depends, for all practical purposes, totally on its relation to, its difference from, its constitutive other'. The Hui and Dongxiang thus differentiate themselves from non-Muslims in general, and the Han (汉) in particular, whom they consider to be 'confused' (*hutu* 糊涂), for a variety of reasons, not least of which is the fact that they are, by and large, atheists.

The Han are seldom referred to by this name, preferring instead to be called *khida* (of Mongolic origin < *kitat* meaning 'Chinese'), which refers to the Han Chinese in general, with no particular connotation. Note that in Mongolic, *kitad* refers to the Chinese in China and not specifically the Han, whereas in Dongxiang, the distinction between 'citizen of China' (*zhōnggŭo rén* 中国人 or *zhōnghúa rénmín* 中华人民) and Han is very clear. Among the other names for the Chinese is *hanmin*, from Chinese *hàn mín* (汉民), which refers to the Han Chinese, particularly those newly settled in the region and living in the outskirts of the county where inter-ethnic cohabitation is more common. To the Dongxiang community, this name has a clear connotation of immigration and foreignness. Among the more educated members of the community, the term *duoshu*, the Chinese *duoshu* 多数 'majority' is also found, in contrast to the term *shaoshu* 少数, 'minority', itself an abbreviation of the Chinese term *shăo shù mín zú* 少数民族, 'ethnic minority'.

When referring to non-Muslims in general, the Dongxiang sometimes use more pejorative terms, such as *nangha* and *boro*. The word *nangha*, the origin of which is not clear, refers both to the Han and to non-Muslims in general. It appears in the term *nangha bidaert*, which means 'teachings and precepts of heterodox religions'. It is therefore a term with strong religious connotations, describing the contrast between Muslims and all non-Muslims. The term *boro* (of Mongolic origin < *boro* ~ *bora* 'grey'), is derived from its original meaning in the DX language: 'grey', 'dark', is a pejorative term that also means 'followers of non-Muslim precepts'. In Dongxiang, it also has the meaning of 'confused, hazy, befuddled'. It should be noted that, in general, all non-Muslims are equated to the Han.

If the Dongxiang define themselves primarily by their contrast to other groups, and particularly to non-Muslims, we might then ask what representations they have for their own group, and what distinctions they make to differentiate themselves from the Hui. Could the demarcation between the Hui and the Dongxiang be no more than a political artifice that has no meaning in the eyes of the Dongxiang?

During the field investigation conducted in 2009, a section of the questionnaire asked about a speaker's identity[81]. They were asked which identity they felt closest to, and could choose from the following options: (1) *dongxiang kun* 'Dongxiang'; (2) *Santa kun* 'Santa'; (3) *Musilin kun* 'Muslim'; (4) *Zhongguo kun* 'Chinese (citizen of China)'. 44% of those questioned said that they identified primarily as ethnically Dongxiang, 9% as Santa, 24% as Muslim and 12% as citizens of China.

The difference between the terms *Santa kun* and *Musilin kun* is one of identity because, as we have explained, Santa is a generic term associated with the Muslim identity of a speaker, and which the Dongxiang often translate into Chinese as 'Hui', another identity-related term. *Musilin kun* is a term of Chinese origin that exclusively describes *Muslim* identity.

Generally speaking, respondents struggled to distinguish between responses 2 and 3, as they considered them to be equivalent. Despite the single choice of response required by the questionnaire, many respondents proposed the combination *Dongxiang Santa kun*, that is, 'Dongxiang-Hui'. However, when asked to choose, they would lean towards one or the other response. The most popular response was number 1, *Dongxiang kun*. This shows that the Dongxiang identity, as defined by the authorities, has been accepted by the members of the community as corresponding perfectly to their ideas of ethnic and identity-related distinctiveness, and that most of the individuals interviewed consider themselves first and foremost as belonging to the category of 'Dongxiang person'.

---

[81] See appendix.

When asked about this, the majority of respondents explained that the only difference between themselves and the Hui (from Linxia) is that they don't speak the same language; the Hui speak Chinese, while the Dongxiang have their own language. However, only 'Dongxiang nationality', the name designated by the Chinese authorities, can be used to define the group as a community speaking a different language, since Santa refers to all Muslim groups, their own included. Today, the Dongxiang refer to other communities who speak different languages by their respective names (Bonan, Monguor, Salar, etc.), which, according to the historical information available, was not always the case (see Section 3.2.). It appears to be a recent phenomenon, emerging at the same time as the authorities recognised these groups as national minorities in the 1950s.

Prior to the PRC, the Dongxiang did not define themselves as a distinct ethnic group; emphasis was on the common nature of Muslim identity. As Sutarinnen (2005) points out, the establishment of the Dongxiang as a national minority, along with the gradual abatement of their geographical isolation over the last 50 years, has encouraged the emergence of a sense of national identity. Although religion continues to play a very important role in their identity, nationality now has the upper hand. By defining themselves in accordance with these new criteria, the cultural aspects that distinguish them from other groups are becoming increasingly important. For the Dongxiang, their language has become an essential element of their identity.

4.2 The Languages and Their Names

There are four main languages in the county of Dongxiang: Dongxiang, Linxia, Beifanghua (including Putonghua) and Arabic. We will expand on their functions and areas of use in the next section.

As previously explained, the Dongxiang group defines itself not only as an ethnic community, but also as a religious one. Their language sets them apart from other groups, but is not the only criterion that serves to define them as a social and ethnic group.

In scientific literature, non-Chinese researchers often refer to the language spoken by the Dongxiang as 'Santa', or 'Santa Mongolian' (Field 1997; Kim 2003). I believe that it is inaccurate to use this name, since it alludes to the Mongolian language of the Santa or, as per the Dongxiang's own definition, the 'Mongolian language of the Muslims'. Chinese scholars, however, use the official name, which explicitly references the Dongxiang group in the name of the language: *dōngxiāng yǔ* (东乡语), 'the Dongxiang language' or (东乡族语) *dōngxiāng zú yǔ* 'the language of the Dongxiang minority'.

The Dongxiang themselves use the Chinese term, *dōngxiāng yǔ*, infrequently, reserving its use exclusively for defining their language to people from other groups. They do sometimes use the term *dongxiang kielien*, a calque of the Chinese term, in which the Chinese word *yǔ* (语) 'language' is replaced by its Dongxiang equivalent, *kielien*.

When talking about their own language, that is, when not defining it in terms of its contrast to others, the most commonly used term is *tuhua*, from the Chinese *tǔ huà* 土话 Lit. 'the local language'. Their language, therefore, is not named in such a way as to define an identity or affiliation to a specific group. As mentioned above, before the PRC, the Dongxiang group formed part of a 'supra-ethnic' whole, so it seems logical that they should perceive their language in terms of locality. The term *tuhua* therefore indicates that, while the Dongxiang are part of a religious community that transcends territorial concepts, their language is a local one.

It must be noted that the Dongxiang do not use the term *tuhua* to refer to any language other than their own, but they do use it when referring to the Dongxiang language spoken by Dongxiang communities outside the county, for example, by the Dongxiang community in Xingjiang. The term is therefore a key element in identifying a community, the Dongxiang, with a language of its own.

Although the Dongxiang community was established solely on the basis of its common language at some point, this state of affairs no longer holds true. As mentioned above, the influence of Chinese is increasing, to the extent that some Dongxiang have become exclusively sinophone (generally using Linxia and other north-western varieties). As a result, the notion of identity can differ, depending on the speaker: for the Dongxiang whose first language is Dongxiang, identity (in terms of contrast) is based on language, whereas the identity of the Dongxiang whose first language is Chinese is based on their official status, their location, and its contradistinction to the territories of China's other ethnic communities. Hence, there is also a territorial aspect to Dongxiang identity. However, as our study is focussed on the Dongxiang whose mother tongue is Dongxiang, we will not expand on the issue of territoriality here. So far as Chinese languages are concerned, at a local level, bilinguals with little or no education only know *Hézhōu huà* or *Línxià huà*, the language spoken by the Hui of the region. They very rarely use the name 'Linxia language', and instead use the term *hanhua* (from the Chinese *hànhuà* 汉话), literally meaning the Han language. This name connotes a degree of sinicisation, which can occasionally be regarded as derogatory by some speakers. As a result, some of them believe that the Linxia Hui are linguistically sinicised Muslims (*hàn huà le* 汉化了), or even that the Dongxiang language spoken in some parts of the county has become sinicised. Given the sense of cultural and religious proximity that exists between the Dongxiang and the Hui, the use of this term seems paradoxical. It is important to note that, in spite of the fact that *hanhua*, the 'Han language', alludes to a sinicisation of the Hui, the Dongxiang have never expressed an attitude of superiority over this group, nor do they feel that they are the inheritors of a purer or more untarnished culture than the Hui, as could have been the case. There would appear, therefore, to be a dichotomy between ethnic/cultural identity and linguistic representation. In other words, the 'sinicised' language of the Hui is not an indicator of their degree of sinicisation in terms of identity or culture. The Chinese language is also called *khida kielen*, (from Mongolic < *kitat* 'Chinese' and *kelen* 'language'), a generic term of Dongxiang origin that makes no distinction between Chinese dialects or languages.

Generally speaking, the Dongxiang do not make a clear distinction between *huà* 话 'speech, dialect', which connotes a local, geographically defined variety, and *yǔ* 语 'language', which implies a more global variety spoken by a larger number of speakers. This is due to the fact that some speakers' awareness of the world is limited to the county of Dongxiang and the Linxia region; as these speakers don't necessarily have contact with anyone speaking varieties other than their own, they don't need to have a name for them. Some speakers are not even familiar with the term *hàn yǔ* 汉语 'Chinese language', only knowing the terms *hàn huà* 汉话 or *khida kielen*. Hence, there is an association between, and a conflation of, the various varieties of Chinese. This phenomenon is not unique to the Dongxiang community, but is widespread across the whole of China, even in scientific circles, where linguists, even those interested in language contact research, often make no distinction between the various varieties spoken. One possible reason for this is that, because of national unity, the authorities attempted to bridge the linguistic divide between the various language communities by creating the standardised variety, Putonghua, in the 1950s. Some even believed that this would lead to the expunging of local dialects and varieties, resulting in the creation of a national, all-embracing language community (Zhou 2003).

For educated speakers (at least high-school level), the term *fāng yán* (方言) 'dialect' is more commonly used. It is used primarily to refer to Linxia, but has a more general meaning in Putonghua and could potentially be used to describe any other Chinese dialect. As the language of education is Putonghua (see Section 4.4.1), awareness of the two varieties among educated people is clearer in terms of contrast to each other, not only in respect of the linguistic differences, but also regarding the domains and spheres of language use. Putonghua is used mainly in schools, for writing and in some highly formal oral contexts, whereas Linxia is used more informally. Among speakers who have not had access to education, some gain an awareness of these dialectal differences through working in places more distant from Dongxiang, particularly in Lanzhou (see Map 1), where the local variety, the Lanzhou dialect, is spoken instead of Linxia.

In general, Dongxiang speakers consider all Chinese languages other than Linxia to be the standardised variety of Putonghua. For example, the Lanzhou variety is equated to Putonghua, even though the linguistic differences between the two are relatively substantial, with the former being classified in the Lan Yin Mandarin (兰银官话 *lán yín guān huà*) sub-branch (Mo and Zhang 2009). Similarly, in some parts of Gansu, most notably in the areas around Dingxi and Tongshui, the variety of Chinese spoken is Zhongyuan Mandarin (中原官话 *zhōng yuán guān huà*), or Central Plains Mandarin, which differs from the other northern varieties.

Also, many speakers who think they speak Putonghua are in fact using a kind of linguistic compromise, combining different varieties of *guānhuà* (官话), also known as *beǐfānghuà* (北方话), meaning 'northern dialect', with Linxia. Thus an amalgam of Putonghua, Linxia and northern dialects has arisen through speakers' limited awareness of the varieties that they use.

Arabic, meanwhile, is still referred to by its original Chinese name, *alaboyu* (from the Chinese *ālābóyǔ* 阿拉伯语), 'Arabic language'.

In summary, then, the Dongxiang identity was historically established on the basis of language, then of religion, and finally, after 1949, of ethno-nationality as defined by the communist authorities. Elements external to the

Muslim community are generally identified as Han. The Chinese language is thus representative of elements outside the 'national' community, that is, the Dongxiang group, but not necessarily representative of elements outside the religious community, as Hui Muslims are Chinese speakers.

We can say, therefore, that the relationship between languages and identity is a complex one: while the notion of Han refers first to non-Muslims and then to the Chinese language and, potentially, to Putonghua, for those speakers able to identify this variety, the Chinese language, and Linxia in particular, does not refer to non-Muslims, but to micro-social elements external to the community.

4.3 The Dongxiang Linguistic Community

4.3.1 The development of the multilingual community

Above and beyond any perceptions that speakers may have of the languages they use, there are four main languages of communication in Dongxiang County today: Dongxiang, Linxia, Beifanghua and Putonghua. For the majority of speakers, Dongxiang is the main vernacular language, whereas Linxia, as in the rest of the region, is the main vehicular language spoken in the county. Dongxiang is therefore the mother tongue of most speakers, and Linxia the second language. Putonghua has no communicative function as such, since it is mainly used for official communications, as a taught subject in schools, and in the media. It is seldom used outside these contexts. As we have already noted, most speakers have only a passive knowledge of the language (they are able to understand it, but not speak it), and when they do speak it, they use a linguistic compromise, a mixture of the various northern dialects, that we refer to as *Beifanghua*. *Beifanghua* is used to communicate with non-Linxia speakers, who are therefore not native to the region. In addition to these languages, there is a sociolect with a religious function: Arabic.

The presence of these languages is the result of contacts with different populations at various times in history. A lack of historical information and documents on the subject means that we cannot expound with any certainty the Dongxiang linguistic community's various stages of mutation. However, cohabitation with the Chinese speakers, and particularly the Hui, allows us to suppose that these changes occurred gradually. Bao (2006) establishes three periods of contact, which we will adopt and expand on here: (1) Monolingualism; (2) The emergence of Linxia and (3) The Development of the bilingual community.

The first, monolinguistic period occurred between the time of the group's formation during the Yuan dynasty (1206–1368), and the Ming dynasty (1207–1644), when heavy Han immigration to the Dongxiang region began to significantly influence the existing pastoral society, completely transforming it into an agricultural one.

The second period occurred between the Qing dynasty (1644–1911) and the Republic of China (1911–1949), more or less corresponding to the period in which Linxia first appeared. Indeed, it was at this point in history that mass immigration to the Gansu region accelerated, thereby intensifying contacts with the Han (see Section 3.1).

Many Han integrated into local populations, giving rise to the first signs of bilingualism. The year 1735, which saw the end of the state monopoly on the trade in tea and horses[82], marked a turning point in the history of the region: Hezhou (now Linxia) became one of the northwest's main centres of free trade, and inter-ethnic trade grew steadily. A new language of communication emerged: Chinese, or what is now known as Linxia. It was during this period that Islam split into different sects; the spread of Islamic thought intensified, strengthening the contacts between the Hui and the Dongxiang.

Finally, the third period, from the founding of the Republic of China (1911) to the present day, represents the final stage in the development of the bilingual community. During the time of the Republic, government authorities mandated the learning of Chinese in religious education. As the Dongxiang language lacked terms in this domain, having previously borrowed them from Persian and Arabic, they were thus obliged to borrow them from Chinese (probably the Linxia variety), thereby furthering the imposition of Chinese loan words into Dongxiang and, to a certain extent, encouraging bilingualism.

Between 1949 and the end of the 1990s, geographical proximity and the isolation of Dongxiang County incentivised the learning of this variety as a second language, leading to the consolidation of bilingualism among a large sector of the community.

82 See Jollife 2007.

Since the mid-2000s, the development of infrastructure and education, along with economic liberalisation and the concomitant improvement in geographical accessibility, have led to an increase in the use of *Beifanghua* or Puntonghua in Dongxiang County, thereby contributing to the emergence of a multilingual community.

All these historical factors contribute to our ability to understand the evolution and intensity of language contacts between the various groups, and explain the transformation into the complex linguistic community that we see today.

It is my view that language contacts with Chinese can be divided into two broad categories: historical and modern.

Indeed, the extensive spread of Linxia during the periods we have just discussed can be described as historical bilingualism, since it has existed since ancient times. As the Dongxiang were geographically isolated and keen to maintain their cultural distance from non-Muslims, their language and the Linxia variety were, for an extended period, in almost exclusive contact; from this situation arose the reciprocal influence of the two languages. These contacts resulted in Linxia having a profound influence on Dongxiang, both phonologically and lexically.

Today, thanks to increasing contacts with external populations, the proliferation of new technologies, the increasingly common acquisition of televisions and the development of education, the influence of *Beifanghua* and Putonghua at the local level is becoming significant. These contacts embody the era of 'modern contact'.

As we mentioned in the previous section, mastery of Putonghua is rare among Dongxiang speakers, who instead use a linguistic compromise that can be described as a northern dialect. Hence, when using the word 'Putonghua' in this section, we will be referring to both this variety and to northern dialects in general, that is, to Beifanghua.

4.3.2 Distribution of plurilinguals

The first study relating to the distribution of bilinguals in Dongxiang was undertaken in 1958 (Chen 2006[83]). For the most part, this study took a geolinguistic approach. It is, incidentally, the only comprehensive study on

[83] Chen does not cite the source of this study.

the distribution of the bilingual population, covering the entire county, ever conducted. According to this study, in the late 1950s, the population could be divided into three zones. The first zone includes the villages of Wangji (汪集), Sijia (四甲), Mianguchi (免古池), Dashu (大树), Luomu (罗穆) and Pingshan (平善). In this zone, only 13% of the population could hold a conversation in Chinese. In the second zone, encompassing the villages of Suonanba (锁南坝), Chuntai (春台) and Pingzhuan (坪庄), 33% of the population spoke Chinese. The village of Suonanba, where bilingualism is now even more common, is a special case in this second zone. This study confirms that in Suonanba, two languages were also used: the general population communicated in Dongxiang, whereas Dongxiang administrative officials spoke Chinese, even with their families, and all non-Dongxiang people also spoke Dongxiang (Chen 2006: 98). Finally, the third zone covers the villages of Baihe (百和), Tangwang (唐汪), Daban (达板), part of the village of Ketuo (科妥), Dongling (董岭), Hongta (红塔), Hongya (红崖), Hetan (河滩), a small part of the village of Guanbao (关堡) and the outer parts of the abovementioned villages of Luomo and Pingshan. In this zone, 93% of the population were able to communicate in Chinese. Around 42% of the total Dongxiang population in the county could hold a conversation in Chinese.

The results presented in this study raise several issues about its methodology. Firstly, no information is provided on the sample of speakers (number of speakers, sex, age, ethnicity, level of education, etc.), which makes it impossible to accurately interpret the figures or to assess whether they are representative of the sample alone, or whether the study was conducted systematically across the entire community and/or population. Furthermore, no details are provided about the team that collected the data, or the methods used to collect it (interviews, questionnaires, etc.). Were only scientists involved, or were they accompanied by officials? What was the ethnicity of these officials? The factors pertaining to these questions may have significantly influenced the results of the study. Moreover, no mention is made of the variety of Chinese in question (Linxia, Beifanghua, or both), which raises a major issue regarding the subject of the study, even though we can guess that, at that time, it would have essentially been Linxia. Nor is there any indication of what the assessments of speakers' levels of Chinese language proficiency correspond to (passive understanding, average conversational level, reading comprehension, etc.), which means that these figures can only be interpreted as loosely indicative.

In his work on the vitality of minority languages in China, Huang Xing (2000) states that bilinguals accounted for 53.44% of the total Dongxiang population, monolinguals for 34.39%, and speakers of another language (without providing further details) for 12.16%. Huang Xing provides neither any specific indication of his sources[84] nor the varieties of Chinese covered by his study.

In subsequent field surveys conducted as part of research into schooling in Dongxiang, researchers consistently address the issue of the distribution of bilinguals from a predominantly geographical standpoint. They all show that the number of plurilinguals increased significantly between 1958 and 1980. Ma Guozhong (2004) conducted a study of pupils aged from 7 to 11, which revealed that 63.5% of children in riverine areas could translate into Chinese the hundred or so words presented to them, whereas only 1.75% of children in mountainous areas could do so. Li and Li (in Ma Guo Zhong 2004) report that, excluding the four towns (*zhens*) of Suonanba, Tangwang, Daban and Hetan, where the Dongxiang live alongside the Han and the Hui, in the other three towns and the twenty 'purely' Dongxiang villages, Dongxiang is both the mother tongue of the majority of the population and their main language of communication. Once again, the researchers provide no details about the varieties of Chinese in question, nor do they comment on the level of linguistic competence of the speakers interviewed. Moreover, the survey does not specify whether the analysed data was derived from written or oral sources. It should also be noted that translation competence is not always reliable and may not necessarily reflect the linguistic competence of an interviewee.

Qi (2004) attempts to overcome this issue by conducting a survey of plurilingualism in the village of Lao Zhuang (老庄村), one of the twenty isolated villages mentioned above, whose inhabitants do not live alongside the Han or the Hui. His survey categorises speakers in accordance with their level of Chinese language proficiency, based on their oral output. The results are summarised in Table 6:

---

84 Huang Xing (2000: 9) provides a table collating figures on China's monolingual and bilingual minority populations, and indicates that some of these figures were taken from McConnell, Tan Ke Rang (1997).

Table 6: Chinese linguistic competence among the population of Lao Zhuang village

Age category		7–14	7–14	15–64	15–64	Over 65	Over 65
	Total	Total no.	Female	Total no.	Female	Total no.	Female
1. Understands little or no Chinese	100	32	17	61	43	7	5
2. Can hold a simple conversation in Chinese	59	9	3	47	26	3	1
3. Speaks and understands Chinese	43	4	1	37	4	2	0
Total	202	45	21	145	73	12	6

These figures show that 43% of those aged 15 years and over understand little or no Chinese. Females account for over 70% of this category. However, among the partially bilingual (category 2), females account for half of the speakers. And finally, among the fully bilingual (category 3), females account for only 10% of the speakers. Unfortunately, even though Qi (2004) does explore speakers' levels of linguistic competence, and briefly outlines the methodology of the survey, other problems remain. Once again, the variety of Chinese to which the survey pertains is not recorded, which makes interpreting the results problematic. More thought could have been given to the evaluation of competence levels, as the categories established for the study are unclear and are subject to the interpretation of the researcher alone. Furthermore, this study represents the situation in the village of Lao Zhuang, and thus cannot be taken to reflect that of the county as a whole. We should also note that the results suggest the existence of a social dimension to the issue (female monolinguals outnumbering the males, etc.); this has not been examined at all. If we wish to maintain the geolinguistic approach to exploring the distribution of plurilingual speakers, we should acknowledge that, while the three geographical areas established in 1958 are still valid today[85], the proportion of bilinguals has increased significantly and therefore the

[85] Ma Guozhong, personal communication (2010).

categories of speaker on which we might focus have also changed. Indeed, owing to various incidences of migration and sinicisation in certain, specific parts of Dongxiang, most notably in the riverine areas bordering the county, the situation has evolved significantly, with areas populated by people whose mother tongue is a variety of Chinese (Linxia or Tangwang) having emerged in the east and west of the county. Not only are these areas predominantly sinophone, but it can also be said that Dongxiang is almost no longer spoken in them; the lingua franca and vernacular is now a variety of Chinese that closely resembles Linxia. There has therefore occurred, more or less recently, a language shift. Once again, a lack of historical data makes it impossible to determine whether this shift was gradual, or abrupt.

By contrast, there are some places in which Dongxiang remains the mother tongue of the majority of speakers, where it is the vernacular but not the lingua franca; in these places, Linxia-Dongxiang bilingualism predominates.

Finally, there are areas in which Dongxiang monolingualism is still very common, but only among a certain category of speakers, particularly women. This does not necessarily mean that monolingualism is dominant, however, as most of the men and younger people can speak one or more varieties of Chinese. Age is also an important factor and must be taken into account; young children and pre-adolescents tend to be less proficient in the various varieties of Chinese because they have not yet been exposed to them. However, once they reach working age, their mobility increases significantly and they encounter people who speak languages other than their own; this is how they acquire knowledge of Chinese languages.

Based on these elements, my observations in the field, and data collected from speakers, I have created the map below, which provides an approximate reflection of the current distribution of plurilinguals[86] (map 2).

The areas of Chinese monolingualism (Linxia or its derivative varieties) are mostly found in the towns and villages on the borders of the county, in the riverine areas (except in the southeast), that is, Dongling, Tangwang, Daban, Gongbei, Baihe, Guanbao and Dongyuan. These areas are described by Dongxiang residents as sinicised (*hanhua* 汉化), even though not all of the inhabitants speak only Chinese (one or more varieties).

86 A systematic study of all the villages would be required in order to create a database enabling determination of the exact proportion of speakers in each category.

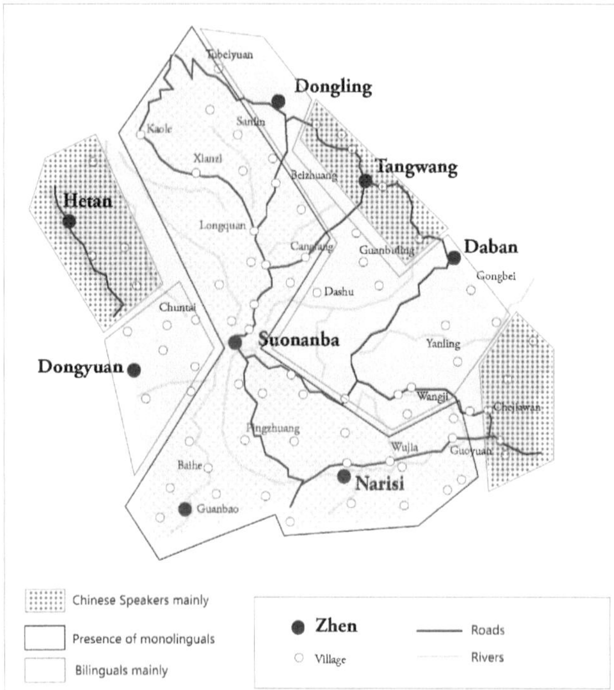

Map 2: Current distribution of speakers in Dongxiang Autonomous County.

4.3.3 The linguistic community and factors in contemporary language acquisition

The acquisition of these various languages is usually gradual and follows an established order. Dongxiang is the speaker's mother tongue (L1), acquired in childhood; Linxia is acquired later (L2) and finally comes Putonghua, a language learned later in the speaker's life (L3). Based on my observations, there are three possible situations within the Dongxiang linguistic community: Dongxiang monolingualism, Dongxiang/Linxia bilingualism and Dongxiang/Linxia/Putonghua-Beifanghua trilingualism.

Once again, to date, there has been no study covering the whole county. Furthermore, the question of language proficiency comes up repeatedly (is passive understanding sufficient to qualify someone as bilingual, etc.). I have not attempted to answer these questions, but left it to the speakers to judge for themselves whether they were monolingual, bilingual or trilingual, without delving into considerations of language proficiency. The purpose of this study was not to report on the multilingual situation in Dongxiang County, therefore I did not conduct a comprehensive and systematic survey of the entire population. However, for the purposes of updating the available data, I carried out part of the field survey using a sample of speakers, as a result of which I was able to identify trends in the distribution of monolinguals, bilinguals and plurilinguals. The survey was conducted in 2009, in the following towns and villages: Daban (达板), Wangji (王集), Suonanba (锁南坝), Beiling (北岭), Longquan (龙泉), Dongling (东岭), Baihe (百和), Heishishan (黑石山), Maomao (毛毛), Nalesi (那勒寺), Yanling (沿岭) Dongling (董岭), Zhaojia (赵家) and Macheng (马城) (see Map 2). The aim of this survey was to provide an account of the sociolinguistic diversity that exists between the various areas of Dongxiang County (urban-rural and mountainous-riverine), which is why I endeavoured to diversify the survey locations as much as possible. Interviews were conducted on a random basis, that is, as and when I met people, and by going door-to-door. This survey was conducted with the help of a female Dongxiang guide, which enabled us to gain access to the homes of speakers, where the majority of interviews took place. Interviews were conducted with 107 people, broken down as shown in Table 7.

Table 7: Breakdown of speakers interviewed, by village

	Men	Women	Total
Suonanba	5	7	12
Beiling	7	10	17
Wangji	5	1	6
Daban (including Gaoshan and Talawu)	12	10	22
Heishishan	4	2	6
Longquan	5	3	8
Yanling (Hexi):	1	5	6
Dongling	2	4	6
Baihe	4	3	7
Macheng	3	6	9
Narisi	2	6	8
TOTAL	50	57	107

From the data collected, I have created categories that account for a speaker's sex, age, education and the type of area in which they live. The "urban area" and "rural area" categories correspond to the inhabitants of towns and other villages respectively. The "educated" category corresponds to those speakers with an education up to at least the third year of primary school. The results are summarised in Table 8[87]:

Table 8: Breakdown of speakers in 2009

Category	Monolingual	Bilingual	Plurilingual	Educated	Total
Men	1	7	42	28	50 (= 46.7%)
Women	19	21	17	11	57 (= 53.3%)
Rural area	17 (incl. 17 women)	13 (incl. 6 women)	22 (incl. 7 women)	10	52 (= 48.6%)
Urban area	3 (incl. 2 women)	16 (incl. 15 women)	37 (incl. 10 women)	29	55 (= 51.4%)
Under 30	7	10	38	35	55 (= 51.35%)
Between 30 and 50	8	13	12	4	33 (= 30.85%)
Over 50	5	5	9	0	19 (= 17.8%)
Educated	0	3 (incl. 1 woman)	36 (incl. 10 women)		39 (= 36.45%)
Total	20 (= 18.7%)	28 (= 26.1%)	59 (= 55.2%)	39 (= 36.45%)	107 (= 100%)

According to the results obtained, 84% of men are at least trilingual, 14% are bilingual and 2% are monolingual. 37% of women are bilingual, 33% are monolingual and 30% are plurilingual.

Around 85% of monolinguals are women living in rural environments, across all age ranges combined[88]. 71% of bilingual women and 59% of plurilingual women live in urban environments.

Around 74% of educated speakers are men. 89% of educated men are plurilingual. 91% of women live, or were living, in an urban environment

87 The figures shown in the various categories of Table 8 are not proportional to the figures for the total population.

88 It should be noted that the three female monolinguals were interviewed in the village of Narisi, which, despite being considered an "urban area" due to its size, is very isolated and remains one of Dongxiang's most remote villages.

while being educated. 59% of plurilingual women and 62% of plurilingual men have attended school.

These figures show us that:

1. The majority of monolinguals are women in rural areas (85% of monolinguals surveyed).
2. Speakers are predominantly at least bilingual (81.3% of speakers surveyed).
3. There are significantly more plurilingual men than there are plurilingual women (71% against 29%).
4. The school enrolment rate is highest among the under-30s, accounting for 90% of educated speakers.

Geography, sex and, to a lesser extent, education and age are all determining factors in the language acquisition process.

Based on my observations, and on data collected from speakers, there are four main tools for acquiring Chinese languages: the linguistic environment, education, workforce mobility and access to the media.

The linguistic environment is the primary tool for the acquisition of Linxia. The streets, the shops, and meeting people from outside the community, or those who don't speak Dongxiang, are the principal means of acquisition. We can say that this tool is contingent on the speaker's sex and where they live. Indeed, men enjoy far more freedom than do women, as their capacity for mobility and opportunities to interact with other men are greater than those of women. Furthermore, the environment also plays a role; urban areas have more places to meet (shops, promenades, marketplaces, etc.), whereas in rural areas, only the street performs this role and cannot be said to represent a regular thoroughfare for speakers from outside the community.

Education is a tool for the acquisition of Linxia or Putonghua, but is dependent on the teacher's level of education and background[89]. Here again, the area in which a speaker lives is a significant factor, as the better-educated teachers are predominantly found in urban areas. In rural areas, Linxia is the most common teaching language. Furthermore, Linxia-speaking Hui live in

89 In some rural villages, it was noted that Dongxiang was the only language used for teaching.

urban areas, so their children mix with Dongxiang children who, through this contact, learn Linxia from them.

Workforce mobility is the tool for the acquisition of both Linxia and Putonghua, as the ability to acquire either variety is dependent on a speaker's temporary place of work. However, I was not able to gain an in-depth understanding of the extent of this phenomenon since, by definition, the vast majority of mobile workers are outside Dongxiang.

In a very relative sense, for male speakers, the sermons given in mosques can also be a tool for the acquisition of Linxia. Of course, this once again depends on the environment in which a speaker lives. Beyond the purely religious aspects, traditionally, an imam must be invited, by the community, to preach in a particular mosque of a given village before he can settle there. The salary on offer thus varies considerably from one rural or urban environment to another. Generally speaking, the more educated an imam is, the more internships he will have completed in the larger surrounding mosques (such as those in Linxia or Lanzhou), thus the more likely he is to have acquired Linxia and the higher the salary he can expect. As rural communities tend to be poorer, they are not able to afford an imam whose reputation is good and whose salary expectations are high. As a result, the best-trained, Linxia-speaking imams preach primarily in urban areas, where there is greater commingling of speakers and where they therefore tend to mix Linxia and Dongxiang (in addition to Arabic) into their sermons as a matter of course.

Last but not least, media platforms essentially favour, albeit passively, the diffusion and learning of Putonghua. With urban areas benefiting from both better infrastructure and higher incomes, access to television is more widespread than in rural areas. Based on the information I gathered, televisions were introduced to Dongxiang only very recently, with the purchasing of sets only beginning to gain popularity around 2005. Incidentally, in an effort to save electricity, some households that own a television do not even use it.

The results obtained show that language learning in Dongxiang is linked both to the tools and to their availability in the area in which a speaker lives. Urban planning is therefore one of the main factors in the acquisition of Linxia and Putonghua, for the following reasons:

1. Economic development attracts people from outside the Dongxiang community into the towns, primarily traders from around the region,

thereby increasing the opportunities for Dongxiang speakers to interact using Linxia.

2. The diversity of employment opportunities in urban areas leads to increased household incomes, thereby enhancing speakers' purchasing power and granting them greater access to media than people in rural areas.
3. The proliferation of schools and the higher concentration of better-trained teachers in urban centres (towns), due specifically to their more advanced economic development, encourages the learning of Putonghua among educated speakers.
4. Because urban environments are less conservative than rural ones, women in urban areas have more opportunities to learn Chinese languages than do women in rural areas, whether by means of the linguistic environment, education or the media.

The second factor in the acquisition of languages is the sex of the speaker. Worker mobility is not, in fact, a contributing factor to the urban/rural dichotomy mentioned above, as there are just as many mobile workers in urban areas as there are in rural ones[90]. However, as worker mobility is predominantly the privilege of the male population, it is generally not a tool available to women for the purposes of acquiring Chinese languages. This situation is specific to Dongxiang, since in most rural Chinese areas, both parents leave their children with the grandparents, in the countryside, while they move to the cities together to work as labourers.

Similarly, when it comes to access to education, priority is given to boys, so it is not surprising to note that nearly three times as many boys attend school as do girls. However, as mentioned earlier, the urban environment does promote access to education for girls, as evidenced by the fact that 91% of educated, plurilingual women were raised in an urban environment.

Finally, and to a different extent, the age of a speaker is also an important factor in relation to learning Chinese languages, and particularly Putonghua. This is because, first, efforts to increase literacy in Dongxiang only really

90 Once again, there are no figures available that could provide more details on the extent of this phenomenon. These comments are the result of observations made during the field survey.

began in the late 1990s, and second, young people now have access to technologies that either did not previously exist, or were not previously available.

There exists, therefore, a triple dichotomy: urban/rural, male/female and younger/older person. While this explains why the linguistic community is so heterogeneous, it does not allow us to make generalisations about all speakers. However, what our results do show is that knowledge of Dongxiang and at least one Chinese language is widespread, accounting for more than 81% of people surveyed. It can therefore be considered, at least with regard to the speakers whom I interviewed, that bilingualism is predominant within the Dongxiang community.

Language Relationships and Linguistic Representations

As we have seen, the number of bilingual and trilingual speakers has increased over the last 50 years, without actually displacing the Dongxiang language. Today, developments in education, communications, transport and media all indicate a steady increase in the number of trilinguals. This raises the question of the ability of the Dongxiang language to maintain its linguistic vitality in a climate in which Putonghua and the northern dialects are becoming increasingly important, and how we might measure this evolution.

The concept of linguistic vitality aims to measure the continuity of intergenerational transmission of a language, taking into account its numerical weight (number of speakers), its frequency of use, and the number of functions or domains in which it is used (Giles et al. 1977). Building on this concept, Huang (2000) developed a model specific to China and its ethnic minority linguistic communities. He establishes ten domains of language use, assigning a maximum of forty points for each category.

He analyses the linguistic vitality of sixty languages spoken by ethnic minorities in China and classifies them in order of vitality. Table 9 summarises the results obtained for the Dongxiang, Va and Uyghur languages, the figures for which reveal varying degrees of vitality.

If we base our understanding on this study alone, then Dongxiang would appear to be seriously imperilled, but the limits of such a model are immediately apparent. Indeed, the domains that it encompasses relate predominantly to written media, leaving no room for oral production and transmission. Huang justifies this choice by arguing that, according to his observations and analyses, 'the written language has penetrated almost all social domains,

Table 9: Linguistic vitality of the Dongxiang, Va and Uyghur languages

	Dongxiang	Va	Uyghur
1. Administration	4.72	6.66	27.47
2. Legislation	0.83	1.67	26.67
3. Legal field	1.00	4.00	24.00
4. Education	0.00	9.24	34.12
5. Publication	0.00	5.00	40.00
6. Media	0.00	0.00	40.00
7. Art and Literature	0.00	10.00	36.67
8. Religion (incl. sermons)	2.00	14.00	8.00
9. Economy	0.63	1.92	20.30
10. Technology (IT)	0.00	0.00	30.00

which is why, in fact, the linguistic vitality indicators apply to practically all aspects of social life.[91]' (pp. 9–10). However, if there is no written language factor to be taken into account, as is the case with Dongxiang, some domains of use are rendered obsolete, while others are entirely missing from the model. In other words, this model is not appropriate for languages whose traditions are purely oral, which is the case in China not only for many ethnic minority languages, but also for the vast majority of Chinese dialects.

Neither does the model include more subjective factors such as linguistic representations, which play a not insignificant role in the process of language maintenance. This method of classification therefore seems to have little relevance in the case of Dongxiang, although it may be appropriate for other minority languages.

It is our view that linguistic vitality is primarily dependent on the 'linguistic weight' of each language, and that any study should therefore consider both the analysis of the role of languages in their macrosocial context, in accordance with their domains of use[92], and the analysis of language relationships, as defined by speakers' representations of them.

91 «语言文字生活实际上几乎是深入影响到了人们社会生活的所有领域，因此语言活力参和指标也实际上几乎涉及社会生活的所有方面.»

92 "Domain" as defined by Fishman 1968.

5.1 Dongxiang's Galaxy of Languages

Despite the linguistic riches and complex sociolinguistic situations that they can reveal, descriptive models developed by researchers in this subject in China are still uncommon. T'sou's model (1983), although not recent, remains the only one to provide a comprehensive approach to the issue of diglossia in China.

T'sou characterises the general situation in China as one of collective diglossia. He establishes three geographical levels for languages: local (village), regional and national. He also identifies two types of language: High (H) languages, which enjoy a more prestigious status than others; and Low (L) languages, which are considered to be less important, or even less valuable, in comparison to other languages. Traditionally, the H languages are truly regional in character, as they are acquired primarily by minority non-Chinese groups. This H language is spoken in all governmental locations and spheres of activity, including in education, and is acquired later in a speaker's life, whereas the L language is acquired in childhood. As T'sou points out, the first linguistic hurdle that a speaker of an L language must overcome will probably be the regional H language that they are obliged to master before proceeding to learn Putonghua.

The H language is therefore a language "superimposed" on the L language; there thus exists a first, basic relationship between the regional H and the local L languages. The degree of prestige of an H language varies from region to region and is dependent on the influence of the government and the level of economic and urban development of a community. Furthermore, in most of the country, Putonghua is considered the "supreme language" (SL). Consequently, we have a home L language, a regional H language, and a national SL language. Today, the H language, traditionally used in certain domains, is being gradually displaced by Putonghua.

Using T'sou's model to describe the situation of the Dongxiang linguistic community, the L language corresponds to Dongxiang, the H to Linxia, and the S to Putonghua. The number of speakers of each language is a criterion by which we can establish the balance of power and, consequently, define their respective linguistic weight.

Pursuing a similar logic, De Swaan (1993) proposes that we think of languages as the stars in a linguistic galaxy, connected by bilinguals, an idea that he conceptualises in his gravitational model, subsequently adapted by

Calvet (1998). If we start with the Dongxiang community and examine the relationships of the languages spoken at the regional level, we see that the demographic weight of Beifanghua speakers[93] far exceeds that of Linxia speakers, and that the demographic weight of Linxia (and the varieties closest to it) far exceeds that of Dongxiang speakers. Dongxiang and Linxia are interconnected via bilingual speakers, largely from within the Dongxiang community, whereas Dongxiang and Beifanghua are only interconnected via trilinguals (those speaking Dongxiang, Linxia and Beifanghua). The number of Linxia-Beifanghua bilinguals has not been determined, but it would appear that most belong to the Linxia community. The interdependence between languages is not clear, and is primarily related to a speaker's participation in social activities that may, or may not, oblige them to use certain varieties. Thus, Dongxiang language's dependence on Linxia is very strong, its dependence on the northern dialects relatively strong, and on Putonghua, rather weak. By contrast, Linxia's dependence on Putonghua and the northern dialects is rather strong, owing to the triple relationship (regional-national, informal-official and identity-national) that exists between these two varieties, an analysis of which would certainly identify a diglossic relationship[94]. Finally, regarding the gravitational pull between the languages, there are two principal poles: the Linxia pole, which primarily attracts Dongxiang speakers (along with the speakers of other regional languages and varieties), and the Northern dialects (Beifanghua) pole, which attracts both the Linxia and the Dongxiang poles.

We are thus faced with a tripolar situation, in which each language represents a sphere with variations internal to each pole, but whose practices also interact with the other poles and influence them externally (Figure 1).

This is therefore a multi-polar situation, with several languages of attraction and several minor languages.

However, the T'sou and de Swaan models are unable to accommodate another language of the Dongxiang linguistic community: Arabic. Although

93 It is very difficult to accurately estimate the number of Putonghua speakers, as studies by Chinese scientists do not consider the issues of bilingualism and the varieties of Chinese spoken.

94 As the focus of this study is the Dongxiang language and community, we have not explored this question.

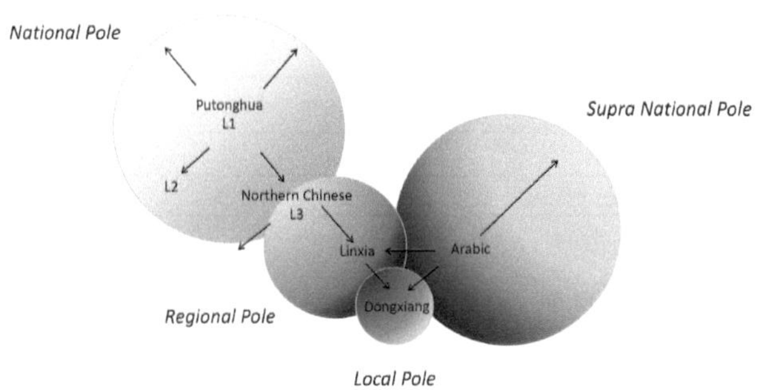

Figure 1: Languages' poles of attraction.

not strictly a language of communication[95], from the perspective of its speakers, this sociolect with a religious function operates as a supreme language, as described by T'sou. There exist, therefore, both a supreme language of communication, Putonghua, and a supra-supreme language with no communicative function. We would likewise expect to find correspondences between the S language of T'sou's model and the Central language of de Swaan's; however, this is not the case, as there is no simple relationship between the languages. Nor does the gravitational model allow Arabic to be included, since this language has no real communicative function, and there is no place for bilinguals, as speakers do not have sufficient linguistic competency in this language to be considered bilingual. Therefore, in order to describe and understand the relationship between them, we must turn to a model that enables analysis of the functional use of languages.

5.2 Roles and Domains of Language Use

Ferguson (1959) defines diglossic situations as needing to satisfy nine features, the first of which is the functional specialisation of the use of languages. Fishman (1971) uses these features as the basis for his introduction of the notion of *domain*. In the case of Dongxiang, this specialisation does not seem obvious, as several languages may follow one another in certain communicative functions (Table 10).

95 Arabic is primarily used in a religious context (see section 4.3.1).

Table 10: Attribution of languages by social-behavioural domain

	Domain ↓ Language→	Dongxiang	Linxia	Putonghua	Arabic
1	Family language	+			
2	Language with peer group	+	+		
3	Non-religious literature			+	
4	Religious literature		+		+
5	Correspondence			+	
6	Contact with local authorities	+	+		
7	Contact with regional authorities		+		
8	Contact with national authorities			+	
9	Contact with traders	+	+		
10	Sermons/worship	+	+		+
11	Basic education	+	+		
12	Secondary education		+	+	
13	Informal education	+	+		+
14	Media			+	
Total number of domains: 14		7	9	6	3

Putonghua appears to fulfil a set of stable and exclusive of functions, primarily associated with governmental activities at the national level, and everything that falls within the realm of written production. Dongxiang fulfils one function exclusively, that of the household language. All other language functions that can be performed by Dongxiang can also be performed by Linxia. Linxia, Dongxiang and Arabic are always associated with other languages within the same communication domain. And finally, the role of Arabic is confined to the intimacy of worship (sermons and personal prayer). We make the observation that, although the language that is used in the greatest number of domains is Linxia, this does not mean that it is the language with the highest frequency of use. Table 11 correlates the domains with their respective relationships-roles and places (Fishman 1986). The single arrows (→) indicate unilateral discourse and the double arrows (↔) indicate mutual interactions.

Table 11: Breakdown of interactions by domain, relationship-role, place

No.	Domain	Relationship-Role	Places/Times
1	Household language	(Intra-familial relations, friendships) Parents ↔ Children ↔ Friends	Home
2	Language with peer group	Friends ↔ Friends ↔ Neighbours	Street
3	Non-religious literature	Ø → Pupils	School
4	Religious literature/ writing	Ø → Imam, clergy	Mosque
5	Correspondence	Individual ↔ Individual	Home
6	Contact with local authorities	Individual ↔ Individual ↔ Neighbours	Home (neighbourhood); local institutions
7	Contact with regional authorities	Authorities ↔ Individual	Official/local institutions
8	Contact with national authorities	Members of local institutions ↔ Authorities	Official institutions
9	Contact with traders	Individual ↔ traders	Market, shops, urban area
10	Sermons/worship	Imam, clergy → Worshippers → Ø	Mosque/home
11	Basic education	Teacher ↔ Pupil	Primary school
12	Secondary education	Teacher ↔ Pupil	Middle/secondary school
13	Informal education	Imam ↔ Pupil	Mosque
14	Media	The world → Individual	Home

Looking at these two tables, we can see very quickly the kinds of problems such models might pose when applied to the Dongxiang linguistic community. First of all, the issue of illiteracy is all too evident. Indeed, taking only our own sample population (see Table 7), only 36% of those surveyed are literate Chinese speakers[96]. Very few speakers are able to read any substantial output with Chinese characters, such as a newspaper.

Moreover, religious literature, in both Linxia and Arabic, is accessible only to a small part of the population, it being the exclusive preserve of members of the clergy (see Section 2.2). The domains of literature and written production are therefore not accessible to the majority of speakers, and thus appear to be minor domains that do not contribute to a general description of the community.

Furthermore, as we have already observed, the diffusion of Putonghua via the media is dependent on whether or not a household can afford to buy a television, a situation which is itself linked to an individual's location (urban/rural). Lastly, sermons as a 'domain' are not directly accessible to women, and thus only reach part of the practising male[97] population.

Although some women do sit in the street and chat with friends and family members, this meeting place is dominated by the menfolk. However, it is considered acceptable for children and older women to join them.

Tables 12 and 13 demonstrate that the use of languages does not operate in terms of domains, but rather in terms of social interactions. That is, the choice of code at the interaction level is determined by the interlocutor and whether they are from within or outside the community, and not by the interactive situation. Furthermore, language relationships relate to oral production, since written production is not available to the whole population.

In terms of domains of use, it can be said that Dongxiang is, on the whole, dominated by the two other varieties of Chinese, but it must also be emphasised that this domination relates to urban life, written literature and media culture, domains which pertain to only part of the linguistic community. Once applied to the reality of the community as a whole, this model no longer makes sense. If we take a male speaker who is fairly representative of the community, that is, middle-aged (around 35 years old), living in a rural

---

96 By 'literate', we mean speakers who can at least read and have had access to at least three levels of primary school.

97 It would appear that, at one time, the recording of sermons on audio cassette tapes was commonplace in Dongxiang, allowing them to be accessed by women; however, to the best of our knowledge, this practice has now been completely abandoned throughout the community.

Table 12: Breakdown of languages by domain for a speaker in a rural environment

	Domain	Language			
		Dongxiang	Linxia	Putonghua	Arabic
1.	Family language	+			
2.	Language with peer group	+	+		
3.	Contact with local authorities	+	+		
4.	Contact with traders	+	+		
5.	Sermons/worship	+	(+)		+

area, illiterate, fairly religious and without a television, then the number of applicable domains of language use is halved. Given his rural environment, I believe that he would have no occasion to interact with regional or national institutions, which either have very little presence in these areas or are represented by members of the local, Dongxiang-speaking community (Table 12). Similarly, the use of Linxia with traders is highly relevant, since this type of speaker is more likely to operate in an urban environment.

If we take this same individual, but place him in an urban context, then the opportunities for interaction in different languages increase and the media domain becomes valid (Table 13).

Table 13: Breakdown of languages by domain for a speaker in an urban environment

	Domain	Language			
		Dongxiang	Linxia	Putonghua	Arabic
1.	Family language	+			
2.	Language with peer group	+	+		
3.	Contact with local authorities	+	+		
4.	Contact with regional authorities		+	+	
5.	Contact with traders	+	+		
6.	Sermons/worship	+	+		+
7.	Media			+	

Thus, we can see that the environment plays a pivotal role not only in the language acquisition process, but also in determining the domains in which languages are used.

The absence of a domain (and, hence, places and opportunities for interaction) for Putonghua in rural areas (Table 12) does not mean that there is a total lack of knowledge of this language: indeed, as we have seen, the predominantly male mobile workforce acquires Putonghua (or varieties of Beifanghua) when travelling outside Dongxiang County. There is, therefore, a relative correspondence between an individual's domain, place and role-relationship and his (or her) relationship with the community outside Dongxiang. In other words, rural speakers have neither the means nor the opportunity to acquire Putonghua locally but, as soon as they leave, they will acquire this variety. What we see, therefore, is that:

1. Several varieties can be used concurrently in the same domain.
2. The heterogeneity of the linguistic community does not allow stable, compartmentalised domains to be established for each language, as can be the case in other multilingual linguistic communities.

Based on these observations, what we have here is a situation of multilingualism with alternative dominant languages, which Platt (1977) defines as a state of polyglossia. In other words, several languages can perform the same function, although it can also happen that a single language is dominant in a particular domain.

In my opinion, the situation is, functionally, one of dual central languages, in terms of both frequency and domain of use. There are not one, but two dominant languages, Dongxiang and Linxia, either of which may gain the upper hand over the other in any given situation or domain, depending on the interlocutor. This corresponds to the situation of majority bilingualism in the linguistic community described above, a perfect bilingualism (with no dominant-dominated relationship) in which the two languages fulfil the same functions. In this situation, Putonghua and Arabic correspond to peripheral functional languages, applicable to particular domains and used only occasionally.

5.3 Linguistic Representations

As I stated previously, Arabic assumes the role of SL in the Dongxiang-speaking world. Indeed, although it has no communicative function, this language enjoys a particularly high status in the eyes of the members of the community, owing to its divine character. Furthermore, whilst it may be thought of as an SL by its speakers, Putonghua is distinguished as a more prestigious variety of Chinese than Linxia, which remains a dialect with no official status. This indicates the existence of a hierarchy of languages. It therefore becomes necessary to understand speakers' perspectives and how they represent the languages, so as to define their relationship with them and thereby make sense of the linguistic landscape. A survey was conducted, using questionnaires and interviews[98], to explore the relationships between Dongxiang and the Chinese languages. Most respondents were unable to distinguish between Linxia and Putonghua, even though they could speak both varieties and grouped them together under the collective name of 'Chinese language'. This conflation is a result of the majority of speakers having only a limited awareness of their linguistic environment. Moreover, although Putonghua is the official language used in schools, many teachers use Linxia, and sometimes even a linguistic compromise of various varieties of northern dialect or Beifanghua, to express themselves in class, thereby reinforcing the amalgam of varieties.

This poses a problem, as a speaker's inability to identify the different varieties involved means that we can neither differentiate their statuses, nor establish the speaker's representations of them. There is therefore, an initial incongruity between the reality of the linguistic community and its linguistic representations.

In the questionnaire, the relationship between languages and their representations was therefore established in terms of the contrast between Dongxiang and the Chinese languages[99]. The survey was conducted among fifty-seven Dongxiang native speakers in the following villages:

---

98 See methodology of field survey by questionnaire (methodology section in the Introduction).

99 Ibid.

Table 14: Breakdown of respondents for the questionnaire-based survey

Village/informant	Men	Women	Total
Suonanba	1	8	9
Beiling	2	6	8
Daban (including Gaoshan and Talawu)	8	2	10
Heishishan	1	2	3
Longquan	1	0	1
Yanling (Hexi):	1	4	5
Dongling	1	2	3
Baihe	1	2	3
Macheng	2	4	6
Narisi	1	5	6
Total	19	35	54

Of the questions asked, nine pertained to their attitudes and their linguistic representations. The first three questions sought to establish speakers' attitudes towards Chinese languages, and their relationships with them, while the other six focused on their attitudes to Dongxiang[100].

The first question was about the use of the various languages and the speaker's representations. For 11.1% of respondents, the use of Chinese implied a higher level of education; for 20.4%, Chinese had to be used because of the requirements imposed by society; for 31.5%, its use was necessary only in response to the requirements imposed by society; 35.2% expressed no opinion, and 1.8% of respondents did not understand the question and did not answer. A third of respondents therefore thought it important to speak Chinese only when a social situation demanded it, suggesting that it was not so much a necessity as a choice imposed by society. The other third believed that it was necessary to speak it in order to have a place in society. The second question looked at the issue of bilingualism, and its development in Dongxiang society as a whole. Of those questioned, 40.75% thought that there was a pressing need for it, 38.9% considered it a natural evolution, 12.9% expressed no opinion, 1.9% believed it to be a bad thing, and 5.55% did not respond. This indicates that the majority of speakers attached importance to

100 See the attached full questionnaire in the appendix.

Chinese languages and were aware that learning them was important for the socio-economic development of their community. The third question asked speakers about their attitude to speaking Chinese. 27.8% of speakers said they very much liked speaking Chinese, 46.3% said they liked speaking it, 3.7% said they didn't much like speaking it; none of the speakers said they didn't like speaking it at all, and 15% expressed no opinion. 7.2% of those questioned were either unwilling or unable to respond. The majority of speakers expressed either a very positive or a positive attitude towards Chinese, which shows that there was no animosity towards the language, despite the fact that it can be associated with the Han, with whom some Dongxiang may be in conflict or identity opposition (see Section 3.1).

The fourth question concerned Dongxiang speakers' feelings about the language. Of the respondents, 22.4% said they were very proud to speak Dongxiang, 29.6% were proud, 12.9% said they were not proud, 31.4% offered no opinion and 3.7% did not answer the question. A little over half the speakers expressed relatively positive feelings about the language, with only a quarter feeling negative about it. The Dongxiang language is therefore an integral part of their identity, whether they are aware of it or not.

The fifth question dealt with the preservation of the Dongxiang language. Approximately, 40.8% of respondents considered it to be a traditional language whose preservation was important, 29.6% thought that it was not an important language and that preserving it was not necessary, 11.1% believed that the language was a hindrance to societal development, 14.8% expressed no opinion and 3.7% either did not understand the question or did not respond.

The sixth question concerned the importance of the Dongxiang language being passed on to children. Approximately, 74.1% of respondents believed that children should be encouraged to speak the language, 14.8% thought that they should not be encouraged to do so, and 11.1% did not answer the question. Once again, there was the feeling, either conscious or unconscious, that the language constituted a legacy whose preservation was important, as it was integral to their identity.

The seventh question was on the subject of bilingual education. Given the choice between education in Chinese and bilingual education, 63% of respondents said they would prefer to send their children to a monolingual Chinese school, 29.6% would prefer to send them to a bilingual school, and

7.4% did not answer the question. This shows that, for these people, not only is it vitally important to learn Chinese, but also that academic study of the Dongxiang language appears pointless.

The eighth question concerned those returning workers or students who, having spent a few years out of the county, refuse to speak in Dongxiang[101]. Of those questioned, 33.3% said they understood this type of attitude, 3.7% found it shocking, 9.3% disapproved of it, 48.1% had no opinion on the matter, and 5.5% gave no response.

The ninth and final question about languages and their representations asked how parents would react if their children could not speak Dongxiang. Approximately, 35.2% of them said they would not mind, 38.9% said they had no opinion, 20.4% said they would not be happy and 5.55% did not answer.

The first observation that we might make when looking at these results is that a significant proportion of respondents either have no opinion or did not answer the questions. The 'no opinion' response scores highest for the first, fourth, eighth and ninth questions, that is, for four of the nine questions. This can be attributed to the fact that the educated Dongxiang population is very much in the minority; the general economic standard is also very low. As a result, language issues are seen as peripheral to their lives, their concerns being of a predominantly material nature.

Generally speaking, the responses suggest that the Dongxiang language is not a conscious component of a speaker's identity. However, attachment to the language is evidenced by the fact that half of the respondents expressed a sense of pride in it (while the other half had no opinion), more than 40% said it was important to preserve it, and 75.1% thought that their children should be encouraged to speak it. Speakers of a language primarily perceive its vehicular functions. Two-thirds of those questioned said they use Chinese and its varieties as a result of the requirements of society, so they see it first and foremost as a social necessity. Similarly, the development of bilingualism, be it natural or peremptory, appears to be a foregone conclusion for 80% of speakers. This indicates the functional perception of Chinese. But at the same time, there is no doubt that there also exists a fairly strong emotional attachment to this language, since only a quarter of speakers said they did not

101 I witnessed this phenomenon during my field surveys, and other speakers also described it to me.

much like, or did not at all like, speaking Chinese[102]. Approximately, 65% of those with very little or absolutely no education, and 82% of educated people, feel either positive or very positive about speaking Chinese. This demonstrates that a speaker's affection for a language is not necessarily linked to education. Generally speaking, I have observed that most uneducated speakers, especially the young, regret their lack of education. This partly explains their affection for this language. On the other hand, speakers' perceptions of different languages cannot adequately explain the hierarchy of their use: that someone likes to speak a language does not necessarily imply that they admire it, nor that they consider it more important than other varieties. For instance, in the case of Dongxiang, three quarters of respondents stated that they encouraged their children to learn and speak it, yet did not feel that it should be taught in school. This corresponds to the domains of use for this language, as established earlier (see Section 4.2), the intra-community communicative function of which is largely limited to the family environment and to friendships. Speakers thus perceive this language as being important emotionally, but of limited social utility.

A closer look at the responses reveals a number of contradictions. The majority of respondents believe that the Dongxiang language should be preserved, yet more than a third think that it would not be a problem were their descendants not to speak it. In other words, these speakers have a genuine sense of attachment to the language, but do not think it necessary to implement measures to preserve it. Despite this attachment, Dongxiang appears 'discredited' and poorly suited to the needs of modern society when compared to the languages of communication used at the regional and national level, namely Linxia and Putonghua, which are, once again, often regarded as being one and the same variety.

In my view, there is a general sense of attachment among speakers towards both Chinese and Dongxiang, whose language functions are perceived and understood primarily in social terms.

Linguistic representations within the Dongxiang community are, as I see it, a reflection of social representations, that is, speakers see the roles and functions of languages in social terms. This corresponds with Calvet's (1998)

---

102 It should be noted that some individuals who claimed to very much enjoy speaking Chinese did not even speak it.

definition of linguistic representations, which he establishes as 'the way speakers think of their practices, how they situate themselves in relation to other speakers and other practices, how they situate their language in relation to the other languages that exist around it.' As Petitjean (2009) points out, this definition refers indirectly to the functions of social representation as defined in social psychology. Through their representations, social actors explain reality by integrating it into a framework that is consistent with their group's values, orienting their behaviours and practices within these shared boundaries. In my view, the way in which the Dongxiang represent the Chinese language corresponds to this reality, as they are aware that not speaking Chinese can, above all, be a hindrance to their own economic development. Hence, there exists a social contrast with the more economically productive sinophone community. Similarly, and for the same reason, most respondents said that they understood bilingualism as both a social necessity and a natural evolution.

Furthermore, according to Pétard (1999), representations also contribute to defining a group's identity and help preserve its distinctiveness. This is why the speakers interviewed emphasised the importance of passing on their language to their children, and also their pride in speaking Dongxiang, which is inherent to their group identity, even if only unconsciously.

Finally, he adds that social representation performs the function of enabling social actors to justify their behaviours after the fact, and to explain why one course of action was chosen over another. It is conceivable that they might abandon their 'identity' language in favour of Chinese, the language required for economic development, which is itself socially encouraged. This attitude is consistent with the Dongxiangs' openness to the world on the one hand, and the linguistic policies implemented and encouraged by the Chinese government on the other (Wang and Phillion 2009). Indeed, contacts with other populations, particularly the Han, engendered by the development of both physical and cultural means of communication, have led them to discover other social values that were not originally their own. As a result, economic success is a growing consideration and is becoming synonymous with social success. This economic success is thus becoming a pretext for the abandonment of the Dongxiang language.

The Chinese language has therefore become a necessity, although Dongxiang still represents an identity. However, the results of the survey indicate that, in terms of representations, the two languages cannot be considered to be in conflict. They are both important to the Dongxiang, but their respective defined roles prevent them from being compartmentalised in an H- or L-language relationship. Dongxiang society appears to be undergoing a transition in which linguistic practices coexist, reflecting a desire to both preserve certain traditional values and to adapt to the more global reality to which its people are becoming increasingly exposed.

5.4 Linguistic Insecurity and Diglossia

As the linguistic weight of Dongxiang is significantly lower than that of the languages with which it coexists, it is legitimate to question how its speakers, numerically overwhelmed by Chinese speakers, feel about using the language, and to ask whether there is a sense of linguistic insecurity within the Dongxiang community.

Francard (1993) defined linguistic insecurity, in the francophone context, as speakers' awareness of a distance between their idiolect (or sociolect) and a language they recognise as legitimate through being that of the dominant class, or that of other communities in which a 'pure' French is spoken, untainted by interference from another idiom, or even that of fictitious speakers who are the bearers of THE standard championed by the educational establishment.

In the case of Dongxiang, awareness of the distance between the mother tongue, Dongxiang, and the 'pure' language, which in this case would be Mongolic, is totally non-existent. As I have already explained, the Dongxiang do not feel close to Mongolians in terms of identity, and the linguistic relationships between Dongxiang and Middle Mongolian are very rarely understood by Dongxiang speakers. There is no 'pure' referent or genetically close, high variety of Dongxiang. The fact that Dongxiang has been 'bastardised' by Linxia[103] thus has no bearing on how speakers feel about their language. Some speakers, however, are aware of the extent of the sinicisation that has taken place in certain places (e.g., the areas on the borders of the county, such as Daban), but are not able to define it in concrete terms. Similarly, certain mountain villages, such as Longquan, are sometimes identified as

103 Significant lexical borrowing, phonological system transfer and syntactic influence are the main phenomena caused by contact with the Linxia dialect. See Chapter 6.

being bastions of an 'unadulterated Dongxiang language', although what constitutes this purity is far from clear. This linguistic insecurity could also apply to the varieties of Chinese, since there is a regional variety (Linxia) and a standardised national variety (Putonghua). However, this relationship is irrelevant since, as I have already made clear, the distinction between these two varieties is made only unconsciously by the majority of speakers. Finally, the educational standard, itself a vehicle for the standard Putonghua variety, does not create a feeling of linguistic insecurity either, as it is a variety of Chinese that teachers themselves have combined with Linxia. It thus appears impossible to establish a feeling of linguistic insecurity since, first, there is no prestigious referent for Dongxiang and, second, the amalgam of various varieties of Chinese makes it impossible to identify the prestigious variety in question. As Bulot and Blanchet (2011) point out, there is a relationship between diglossia and linguistic insecurity. Drawing on multiple studies, they conclude that linguistic insecurity is not automatic for any speaker of a 'minorised' language, but depends on their knowledge of the legitimate language and their awareness of a distance between it and their own variety, two 'knowledges' provided by the educational system. In the case of Dongxiang, limited knowledge of the linguistic environment does not cause insecurity in the speaker.

On the other hand, an absence of linguistic insecurity does not imply an absence of diglossia. Indeed, the fact that speakers have no real negative relationship with either Dongxiang or Chinese might lead us to wonder whether the linguistic landscape is in fact made up of only H varieties (and thus no L varieties). Furthermore, the hierarchy of languages established through analysis of their domains of use (in which languages can be either dominant or dominated, depending on the context) is deconstructed when the analysis of language relationships is reconsidered in the context of representations. Thus, from the speaker's perspective, the oppositional relationship between the L, H and S languages, as defined by T'sou in his model, does not appear to be applicable to the Dongxiang linguistic community. In his model of representations, Calvet proposes an understanding of language relationships based on not only the role of the speaker and their linguistic attitudes, but also the reality of the situation, speakers' self-evaluation of their language practices, their representations of these practices, and what the speakers themselves would like to do. Four types of situation are identified: (1) Evaluative and representative security, (2) Evaluative security and representative insecurity (3) Evaluative insecurity and representative security and (4) Evaluative and representative insecurity. In the case of the Dongxiang community, the three couplets, (1) Awareness/non-awareness (of the linguistic environment), (2) Adherence to/rejection of (the dominant language) and (3) Security/insecurity (regarding the linguistic situation) used to evaluate a speaker's sense of security or insecurity causes certain problems.

Since a speaker's awareness of their own linguistic environment is relative, individuals can clearly differentiate between their mother tongue (Dongxiang) and the language(s) of communication, that is, the Chinese language(s), as they are aware of what they are speaking, with whom, and in what circumstances. However, it seems that speakers find it more difficult to differentiate between the varieties of Chinese, Linxia and Putonghua/northern dialect; they may claim to have no knowledge of a variety while simultaneously speaking it. Such a phenomenon is not exceptional, this kind of representation being observed in similar situations among other multilingual communities. The adherence/rejection couplet also causes some problems because, as we already know, there is not ONE dominant language, but several. The dominant language is not defined in terms of domains of use or by representations, but exists nonetheless, if only due to the pressure exerted on the Dongxiang community by the number of speakers of other Chinese varieties. The criterion is therefore one of reality rather than representations.

Finally, as far as a speaker's self-assessment in a language is concerned, there cannot be said to be any conflict between Dongxiang and the Chinese languages, as they are respectively internal and external to the community. Nor can there be said to exist a clear, representative trend among all speakers concerning their feelings about the linguistic landscape. As previously discussed, given that the educational level of most speakers is very low, and economic survival their prime concern, their reflections on their linguistic environment are understandably limited.

Overview of Contact-Induced Change and Code-Mixing Phenomena

Contact-induced change in Dongxiang has been described in details by Bao (2006; 2017), Min (2018) and Lefort (2013, 2015a,b, 2017, 2020, 2022). Therefore, in this chapter, we will provide only a brief overview of the general characteristics of the Dongxiang language and the features that have been induced by contacts with the Chinese language, in particular with the variety of Linxia, before addressing the issue of code-mixing.

6.1 Phonological Changes

Because of the large amount of Chinese loans borrowed in Dongxiang, the fact that it has been isolated from other Mongolic languages (especially those of the central branch), and that it has not been connected with any form of Written Mongolian, its phonology has been deeply modified. According to Field (1997: 170) 84% of the Dongxiang syllables are shared with those of Linxia Chinese (Hezhou), which shows the importance of language contact in the evolution process of this language.

One of the most important changes in the phonetic system of the Dongxiang language is the lack of vowel harmony, which has probably been lost through the influence of Chinese, and the lack of vowel length. In Middle Mongol, as well as in most Modern Mongolic languages, a distinction between back (*e*, *ü*, *ö*) and front (*a*, *o*, *u*) vowels is observed, while *i* is often neutral. In Dongxiang, both types of vowels can appear in the same word:

barei (< *bari*) 'take'
naogvei (<*noxai*) 'dog'

Middle Mongol did not have long vowels, but an intermediary hiatus (also noted *g* and *h* depending on the sources) which has evolved to long vowel codas [VV] in Modern Mongol (hereunder comparative examples from Khalkha). In Dongxiang, it either has developed to short vowel or diphthongs:

nie [niə] (< *ni'e*) 'to open'; Kh. *nee*
u [u] (< *u'u*) 'to drink'; Kh. *uu*

The other most common phonological changes in Dongxiang as compared with Middle Mongol are summarised below (Field 1997; Bao 2006; Nugteren 2011):

a. Strength/aspiration shifts
khighei [qɯɢəi] < *gakaï* 'pig'

b. Deletion of most non-nasal coda consonants
edou [odəu] < *ebüdüg* 'knee'
lachin [latʂin] < *nabči(n)* 'leaf'
hhangva [haŋɢa] < *haryal* 'dung from animals'
kha [qa] < *ɣar* 'hand'
hhanku [haŋku] < *alqum* 'step'

c. Vowel epenthesis for other non-nasal coda consonants
basi [basi]< *bars* 'tiger'

d. Reduction and elision of vowel
kixie [kiɕie]< *keseg* 'piece'.
melie [məlie] < *emüne* 'front'

e. Final *m* and *l* to *n* or *ŋ*

m > *n*	*gien* [giən] < *gem* 'disease'
m > *ŋ*	*san* [saŋ] < *sam* 'comb'
l >*n*	*kon* [koŋ] < *köl* 'foot, leg'

f. Fronting and backing of vowels
pixie [piɕiə] < *büse* 'belt'

g. Palatalisation of alveolar stops before front vowels
d > *tɕi* *oqiegven* [otɕiəʁəŋ] < *hödken* 'thick'
d > *dʑi* *jiesun* [dʑiəsuŋ] < *deesü(n)* 'rope'

h. Assimilation of first syllable **ï* and **i* by the second syllable vowel ('palatal breaking'):
ï > *u* *chusun* [tʂusuŋ] < *čïsun* 'blood'

i. Assimilation of the middle vowel of tri-syllables:
khudogvo [qudoʁo] < *kïtoga* 'knife' (due to the *a* of the following syllable)

j. Harmonic rounding of the following vowel by the vowel of the preceding syllable:
gholo [ɢolo] < *kola* 'far'
boro [boro] < *böere* 'kidneys'

Among the above, points a) to g) are unique to the Dongxiang language, while points h) to j) are also found in other Mongolic languages, including those of the Shirongolic group spoken in the Gansu-Qinghai area.

6.2 Lexical Borrowings

As mentioned in Section 3.2, the proportion of vocabulary of Mongolic origin and borrowed varies from one study to another, depending on the material and the methodology used. Regarding the Dongxiang language in particular, in Buhe's dictionary (1986), 12% of the 3,830 entries of Chinese origin, including 37% of the adjectives, 55% of nouns and 29% of verbs. Field (1997: 263–267) explains that this number is due to (1) The low cultural knowledge of the researchers, who have not documented vocabulary specific to the Dongxiang people and culture; (2) The collection mean was exclusively translation from Chinese, which has influenced the informant; and (3) Due to the political environment at the time, many administrative and political (now obsolete) terms had to be added to the list of vocabulary. Therefore, although it is a valuable work, Buhe's dictionary cannot be used to fully understand the borrowing phenomena. Based on Ma and Chen's Dongxiang-Chinese Dictionary (2001), Bao Saren (2006) and Kim

(2003) count 34% of Chinese borrowings out of 10,145 entries (including derived nouns, compound pairs and proper nouns), which seems to be a more realistic proportion.

Chinese loaned vocabulary is not limited to a specific lexical field and has penetrated all the lexicon, whether it be modern (*danyen* 'party member' < *daŋjan* 党员), local (*gha* 'small' < *ga* 尕), standard (*kuaiji* 'accountant' < *kuaidẓi* 会计), every day (*beizi* 'cup' < *beidzi* 杯子) or specialised (*jiennao* 'computer' < *dẓiənnao* 电脑) lexicon.

6.2.1 Nouns

From a morphological perspective, borrowed nouns from Linxia Chinese function in the same manner as those of Mongolic origin. In addition to direct borrowings, there are a number of calques and semi-calques, that is to say borrowings in which the meaning and structure of the borrowed language are retained, but the original phonetic form is abandoned. The calques are based on Chinese bi-morphemic words and, most of the time, reproduce this association by combining two morphemes, where only one morpheme is usually used in other Mongolic languages, for example:

(1) *chizhe zhugve* (litt. 'flower-heart') 'pistil' < LX *xuA*^{243}*ɕiŋ*^{243} (花心 litt. 'flower-heart') 'pistil' ; Kh.: *doxiür* (дохиур ᠳᠣᠬᠢᠶᠣᠷ) 'pistil'

Semi-calque is composed of a direct loan associated with a morpheme of Mongolic origin, the new word copies the Chinese bi-morphemic word structure, for example:

(2) *naizi arasun* 'cream' *naizi* < LX *nɛ*^{43}*ʈsɿ* 奶子 'milk' + *arasun* < Middle Mongol *arisun* 'skin' *from naipi* 奶皮 (litt. 'milk-skin') 'skin on boiled milk'. Kh.: *orŏm* (өрөм) 'skin on boiled milk'.

6.2.2 Adverbs

Although the category of adverbs is present in Mongolic languages, the meaning of most Chinese adverbs is expressed with converbial morphology. Therefore, there is a functional gap that has been filled with Chinese borrowings in Dongxiang. The most current borrowed adverbs are temporal ones, with strong lexical value. They include *yihou* 'after' (< *i*^{43}*xou*^{42} 以后), *yizhi* (<*i*^{43}*ʈʂʅ*^{243}一直) 'all the time' and *yibeizi* (<*i*^{43}*pei*^{42}*tsɨ*一辈子) 'always', for example:

(3) bijien <u>yizhi</u> kielie-zhuo, hhe kewon-de echi-zhi shi zui gansan.
1P always talk-PROG 3 child-DAT go-SIM COP most handsome
'We always said he was the most handsome!'

Other adverbs include aspectual adverbs such as *zhishi* < LX *ʈʂʅ*^{243}*ʂʅ*^{42} 只是 'only'; *ijin* < LX *i*^{43}*tɕiŋ*^{243} 已经 'already', *dou* < LX *ʈu*^{243} 都 'all', etc.

As for nouns, borrowed adverbs do not bear any specific morphology.

6.3 Morphological Changes

In Modern Mongolian, Chinese loanwords are completely assimilated and function with the same suffixes as words of Mongolic origin do. The Dongxiang language, however, has developed its own lexical derivation morphology for certain categories of Chinese loanwords.

6.3.1 Borrowed adjectives morphology

Most borrowed adjectives do not bear any additional suffix, and are borrowed 'as is' from Chinese, for example, *putong* < *pŭtōng* 普通 'common'.

However, some adjectives are borrowed from Linxia Chinese together with the marker *-ji* (pronounced *ʈi* or *dʑi* in Linxia), which is the equivalent of Standard Chinese marker *de* 的, for example:

(4) *zhongyaoji* 'important' < *dʐunjao tɕi* 重要的

In Linxia Chinese, one of the functions of the marker *-ji* is to show that the adjective modifies the element it precedes, while in Dongxiang, *-ji* is borrowed together with the adjective with which it forms an inseparable unit.

Other borrowed adjectives are suffixed with the Dongxiang marker *-ni* which can bear several functions, including those of the genitive marker and third person possessor. When it is added to borrowed adjectives in

Dongxiang, it is a calque of Linxia Chinese marker *-ji* which is also the form for the genitive marker, for example:

(5) *fang-ni* 'square' from Chinese *fang-de* 方的

Most monosyllabic adjectives are with *-ni*, which is used exclusively with adjectives of Chinese origin, not with Mongolic ones. Therefore *-ni* is a borrowed adjective derivation suffix and not a grammatical marker (see Lefort 2015b for details).

To summarise, the marker *-ji* is a direct borrowing, and *-ni* is a calque[104]. This point will be further developed in Section 6.6.

6.3.2 Borrowed verbs morphology

Monosyllabic verb ending with a vowel are suffixed with the marker *-yi, for example maoyi* 'to gush' from Linxia Chinese *mao*^{42} 冒 'to gush'. Monosyllabic verbs ending in a consonant are suffixed with *-ji*, for example: *piinji* 'to meet' from Linxia *peŋ*^{42} 碰 'to bump into someone'. In addition to these two forms, there are other suffixes which are used exclusively with verbs of Chinese origin, the most common of which is *-da*, for example, *pienda* 'to fool' from Linxia *piaŋ*^{42} 骗 'to fool'. At last, bisyllabic verbs are associated with the auxiliary *gie* 'to do', for example:

(6) Hhe xuexiao-de <u>caifang</u> <u>gie</u>-le echi-zhuo
3 school-LOC interview do-PURP go-PROG
'She came to make interviews in a school.'

This specific verbal morphology is not rare in Mongolic languages (e.g., Buriat, Dörbed Mongolian, etc., see Bao 2011) and in languages of the world in general (e.g., Belizean Spanish, see Fuller 2020), and are usually referred to as 'Bilingual Compound Verbs' (Myusken 2000: 193–220).

6.3.3 Suffixal reduction in converbial constructions

The Dongxiang language is a chaining clause language, which is characterised by the chaining of several verbs linked together by markers, usually known

104 See Lefort 2015b for full discussion.

as converbs, gerunds or switch event markers in the literature. These markers have two main functions: (1) to determine if the moment in which the action takes place is the same for the two verbs and (2) to specify the semantic and temporal relationship between the two verbs. The lexical value of these markers varies from one another. According to Field (1997: 429), there are seven converbs in the Dongxiang language that fulfil this function:

1. causality marker (CS) *-se* 'so'
2. consecutiveness marker (CONS) *-dene* (*-de*) 'then'
3. purposive maker (PURP) *-le* 'to'
4. immediate marker (IMM) *-senu* 'immediately after'
5. limitative marker (LIM) *-tala* 'until'
6. simultaneity marker (SIM) *-zhi* 'as X, X was happening'
7. integrative marker (INT) *-Ø*

The simultaneity maker *-zhi* shows that the two verbs are part of a single event and action, while the integrative marker demonstrate an greater degree of integration between the two verbs. All these markers have correspondences in other Mongolic languages, but the unmarked integrative has developed under the influence of Chinese calques of directional and resultative constructions[105], leading to the reduction of marked morphology in the Dongxiang language. For example:

(7) ijie-Ø balu-Ø xianzi-de-ne oro-gva-wo.
eat-INT finish-INT box-LOC-REFL enter-CAUS-PFV
'After he ate, she made him go back to the box.'

In the above example, the compound *ijie balu* litt.: eat-finish 'finish eating' is a calque of the Chinese resultative construction LX 吃完 *chʅ*[24]*-wæ̃*[243] litt.: eat-finish 'finish eating' where verbs are unmarked. In this particular clause, the causality or the consecutive converb would be expected on the second verb *balu*. This phenomenon is also found in other Mongolic languages of

105 For a full discussion on claques of directional and resultative constructions in the Dongxiang language, see Lefort (2015a).

the Gansu-Qinghai area which have been influenced by Chinese, such as Mangghuer.

6.4 Function Words

6.4.1 Negations

Most of the Dongxiang negations are inherited from Middle Mongol (prohibitive *bu* < *büü*; irrealis *ese* < *ese,* realis *ulie* < *ülü*) or have developed from Middle Mongol forms (possession negator *wiya*, *wiwo* < *ugui,ügegü*, *ügegüi, ügegün*).

Under the influence of Chinese, the negation system has developed functions which are summarised below:

6.4.1.1 Prohibitive negation bu

Dongxiang prohibitive *bu* is, most of the time, used as in Middle Mongol, that is to say preceding the verb with imperative mood (zero marking):

(8) chi <u>bu jinda</u>, <u>bu weila</u>, chi hai-ne say-zhi arugva, bi sagvi-ne.
2 NEG panic NEG cry 2 shoe-REFL clean-SIM wash 1 wait-IPFV
'Don't panic, don't cry, clean up the shoes, I will wait.' (Lefort 2012)

The homophonic Chinese negation *bu*^{42}不 is used in Linxia as in Standard Chinese, that is to say as an irrealis negation:

尕丫头一点话都不听
kA^{43} ^{3}yA^{243}tou^{243} itiæ χuA^{42} ʈu^{243} pu^{42} tɕiŋ^{243}
little.girl a.little word all NEG listen
'The little girl is not obedient at all' (LXFY: 175)

In Dongxiang, the ascriptive negation *bu* is sometimes used as in Chinese, that is to say as a irrealis negation:

(9) gaga <u>bu xiangxing</u>, azei-ni yidong egve-wo
elder.brother NEG believe elder.sister-3POSS CL bit-PFV
'The elder brother did not believe his sister and bit her'

In this example, *bu* seems to be forming an inseparable unit with the verb it precedes, and, in this particular case, the borrowed verb *xiangxing* (from Chinese *ɕiaŋ*^{243}*ɕin*^{42} 相信). Moreover, the verb is used without the borrowed verb auxiliary *gie* 'to do', which would be expected here. Therefore, this kind of phenomenon would rather be identified as code-mixing compound rather than a grammatical borrowing *per se*. This point will be discussed in Section 6.6.

However, *bu* also appears instead of the realis negation *ese* in pre-verbal position with integrated borrowed verbs:

(10) Enende yang shi khawitu-zhuo, jiu bu guomin gie-zhuo.
here.LOC what COP swell-PROG so NEG allergy to.do-PROG
'This (part) here is swelling, so it is not an allergy'

This shows that negation *bu* is extending its functions through a complex mechanism which can be interpreted in different manners: (1) realis negation *bu* is a direct borrowing from Chinese, which is coincidently is homophonic with the Dongxiang prohibitive negation *bu*. Therefore, Dongxiang negation system features two distinct negations bu_1 and bu_2 or (2) realis *bu* is a calque from Chinese realis negation *bu* which has superimposed its functions on the existing prohibitive negation *bu*.

6.4.1.2 Possession negator wu

Dongxiang has developed a possession negation verb, probably based on Middle Mongol *ugui*[106], which is most of the time, used with the copula *wo* 'to have'. Copula *wo* always expressing action or events that took place in the past:

(11) basi munie zhayasan-de basi-de benshi wu wo. (Buhe 1987:184)
tiger world create-SS tiger-LOC knowledge NEG COP
'After he came to the world, the tiger had no knowledge.'

106 For a full discussion on negation development in Dongxiang and Mongolic languages, see Brosig (2015).

However, in my corpus, *wu* appears as an independent verb meaning 'not to have' and is almost never associated with the copula *wo*:

(12) Ingiese laohu yama banfa wu, mutun doura-de bai-zho.
then tiger what solution NEG tree under-LOC stay-PROG
'The tiger did not have solution and stayed under the tree'

The predicate-final position indicates that it has a very strong verbal value, and in fact, there is no other verb in the clause. Therefore, negator *wu* has developed a temporal (past) value.

Some peculiar use of the negator *wu* is that it can negate verbs, most of them bearing no morphology, and in clauses where the possession value one the lixical level of *wu* is abandoned:

(13) ghua igva ijie wu.
two bowl eat POSS.NEG
'We did not eat two bowls'

This shows that it has fully developed as a realis negation verb, most probably under the influence of the Chinese negation verb *miei iou*[43] 没有, which is also composed of a verb (有 *iou*[43]) and a negator *miei* 没 that can be used alone. It was initially a possession negation verb before developing to a standard negation for past events. Therefore, the use of possession negator *wu* alone in Dongxiang and its development to past verbal negator is a calque from Chinese *miei iou*[43] 没有.

6.4.2 Classifiers

Although measure words are present in all Mongolic languages, there is no category of classifier. However, under the influence of Chinese, Dongxiang (as well as Mangghuer, see Slater 2003: 95) has developed a new category of function words, which is similar to Chinese nominal classifiers[107].

Most of the directly borrowed classifiers in Dongxiang are associated with a borrowed numeral and/or a borrowed noun, therefore the context in which they appear is highly influenced by Chinese, and it appears that the classifier

[107] For a full discussion on the emerging category of classifiers in Dongxiang, see Lefort 2015a.

is borrowed as a single unit with the item it precedes or follows [NUM + CL + N] or [NUM + N + CL]. This point will be developed in Section 6.6.

On the other hand, an independent classifier, *kozi*, seems to function as a general classifier, which can be used with animate beings or inanimate objects, and may co-occur with a numeral and a noun of Dongxiang origin:

(14)	fugierei	bogvo-de-ne	nie	kozi	bazhi	khiche-gva-dene	ese
	ox	bottom-LOC-REFL	one	CL	dung	out-CAUS-SS	NEG
	baozhe-gva-zhuo	gie-ne.					
	fall-CAUS-PROG	say-IMPV					

‘The ox defecated, but the dung didn’t fall out of his backside.’

The classifier itself could be of Linxia origin (< *k’ou*^{43} *tsi* 口子), which is used mainly by people in the expression *liaŋ*^{43} *k’ou*^{43} *tsi ʐəŋ*^{243} 口子人 ‘a married couple’. However, it functions like the general classifier *kə* 个.

6.4.3 Copula *shi*

Dongxiang has borrowed the Chinese median copula *shi* (< *ʂi* 是) ‘to be’, which can be placed after the subject and is used as a topic marker. Its use is optional, and the sentence must, in principle, end with another copula of Mongolic origin, usually the copula *wo* ‘to have, to be’:

(15)	danshi	pese	agu	shi	qin	agu	wu	wo.
	but	again	aunt	COP	blood.parent	tante	NEG	COP

‘But also, my aunt is not my parent by blood.’

There is no fundamental difference between a sentence with or without the copula *shi*, except emphasizing the subject. It can be combined with other verbs in the predicative position which need to bear an aspectual marker:

(16)	ene	shi	bi	ulie	fuya-dene	aghili-ni	agi-zhi	ire-se	chi
	DEM	COP	1	NEG	tie-SEQ	knowledge-ACC	take-SIM	come-PST	2
	yawu-la	wida-se	kien-de	uzhe-gva-ne?					
	go-COND	finish-CAUS	who-LOC	see-CAUS-PFV					

‘If I don’t tie you up and when I come back you’re gone, to whom will I show the knowledge I have acquired ?’ (Buhe 1986)

In Linxia Chinese, the copula *shi* is found in the same type of combinations when it is used in declarative sentences and is combined with a final verb:

(17) 这个衣服是我阿达穿下的. (LXFY 1996:163)
tʂɨ^{42} kə i^{243}fu ʂi ŋə^{43} a^{243}da tʂ'uæ̃^{243} χa ʈi
DEM CL clothes COP 1.POSS father wear RES SUB
'These are the clothes my father wears'

It is not uncommon for the word order of Middle Mongol sentences in Arabic sources to be SVO (and not SOV), which is probably due to language contact (see Rybatzki 2003: 78). Median verbal copulas are also attested, producing a SVOV clause type. In modern Mongolian, the use of the medial copula is not uncommon either, but is limited to the verb *bol-*[108]. However, in Dongxiang the final verb may be omitted:

(18) nie shi chighan mudan, nie shi shira mudan, nie shi hulan mudan.
one COP white flower one COP yellow flower one COP red flower
'One flower was white, another one yellow, and another one red.'

This type of structure is also found in Field (1997), which indicates that it is not a new phenomenon. This calque changes the word order in Dongxiang from SOV to SVO. The word order change is limited to the use of this copula, but is becoming more widespread through code-mixing.

Furthermore, the copula *shi* is also used as a final modal particle to express emphasis:

(19) zhugve dogvun shi.
heart ugly MP
'They were ugly people'

This use of modal particle *shi* is not attested in Linxia Chinese, and therefore should not be associated to a calque. The Chinese copula *shi* and the Dongxiang copula *wo* share some lexical value and can both mean 'to be'

108 *bi bol suragc* litt.: I be student 'I am a student' (Chinggeltei 1991: 492).

or 'to have'. Therefore, they have been associated through semantic and *shi* replaces *wo* in predicate final position.

6.5 Grammatical Borrowings

6.5.1 Manner adverbial *-ji*

The Dongxiang language has borrowed the manner adverbial marker *-ji* from Linxia Chinese *tɕi* 地, which is homophonic with the borrowed adjective suffix *-ji* (< *tɕi* 的).

In Dongxiang, manner can be expressed by duplicating the adjective and adding the suffix *-ji*. It can be omitted most of the time, but is often used with onomatopoeia and duplicated adjectives:

(20)	Ingiese	yanzi-de	kun-ni	pazha pazha-ji	ijie-zhuo,	gie-ne.
	then	courtyard-LOC	man-ACC	gluttonously-MAN	eat-PFV	say-IMPV

'Then, they said that a man was gluttonously eating in the courtyard.'

This is a copy of the adverbial construction found in Linxia Chinese, where the particle *-ji* 地 is also used with duplicated adjectives. Whereas in Standard Chinese the equivalent particle is generally optional with adjectives and obligatory with multisyllabic adjectives expressing condition or state, in Linxia Chinese it is automatically added to all multisyllabic adjectives:

(21) 你炕上还长拉拉地躺下着!

ɳi^{43}	kaŋ^{42}	ʂaŋ^{43}	χæ^{243}	tʂaŋ^{243}lA^{243}lA-tɕi	t'aŋ-	χA-	tʂə
2	kang	on	still	all.length-MAN	lay	RES	DUR

'You are still laying on the Kang!' (LXFY:1996: 165)

The suffix *-ji* in Dongxiang is also used in constructions including native words, for example in *udu udu-ji* '(do something) day after day', *mimi-mama-ji* '(do something) very densely' where the particle has been adopted as an adverbial suffix (Ma and Chen 2001). Some adjectives of Chinese origin may have been borrowed with the Chinese suffix *-ji*, expressing manner, which later became independent. Nowadays, the suffix *-ji* is no longer a simple derivation suffix, specific to words borrowed adjective from Chinese, but an independent suffix that can be used with stems of Mongolic and Chinese origin; it has therefore been grammaticalised.

6.6 At the Edge Between Borrowing and Code-Switching

As we have seen, the influence of Chinese on the Dongxiang language is noticeable in every aspect of the language, and it mostly has been influenced by the local variety of Linxia Chinese. Standard Chinese has also started to influence it recently, but in a different manner. That is why it is important to keep in mind that these are two varieties when analysing code-mixing and code-switching phenomena.

Code-switching is the exploitation of the resources of different languages by bilinguals; it may be motivated by stylistic or social reasons. It refers to the linguistic phenomenon wherein bilinguals or multilinguals switch between two or more languages within the same discourse or conversation, and occurs in stable situations where bilingualism is the norm in the community, which is true for the greatest part of the Dongxiang community (see Chapter 4).

Intra-segmental switching is not considered to be code-switching, but code-mixing. The latter is constituted by the use of words or phrases in an interaction that uses one language as a 'matrix language'. This last definition raises the problem of the use of loanwords integrated into the receiving language, such as Dongxiang. As nouns and adverbs do not bear any morphology, any noun and adverb is potentially borrowable and can be used without conflicting with the Dongxiang word order. Bissylabic verbs, on the other hand, are integrated with the auxiliary 'to do', which also makes any verb borrowable. In other words, that it becomes difficult to define at what point the word or utterance from another code is borrowed from or mixed with the first language. Code-switching and borrowing are therefore distinguished by the frequency with which a word or a syntactic element is used by a monolingual speaker and by its degree of integration. When the word used has completely ousted its native homonym and the grammatical categories that tend to be borrowed no longer conflict with the existing system, then the element can be considered as borrowed, thus integrated. This has led some researchers, such as Myers-Scotton (1993), to believe that the processes of code-switching and borrowing form part of a continuum and are based on the degree of insertion or assimilation.

There are several approaches to defining code-switching, including the Markedness model developed by Myers-Scotton (1993). One of the key concept of the model is the matrix language frame (MLF), whereas bilingual or multilingual speakers select forms from another language to introduce them into a matrix language during the same conversation. In this model, the production-based analysis considers code-switching as a set of processes that operate before the combinatorial level, where word order and structures are realised. It thus establishes the concept of Matrix Language (ML) as opposed to Embedded Language (EL). Both the matrix language and the embedded language have their own sets of morphemes, which function in a grammatical system belonging exclusively to one or the other language. When the matrix language is combined with the embedded language, the morphemes are constructed from both languages, but function only in the syntax of the matrix language.

The Matrix Language Frame (MLF) model is based on four hypotheses: the Matrix Language Hypothesis, the Blocking Hypothesis, the Embedded Language Islands (ELI) Hypothesis and the Implicational Hierachy of Embedded Language Islands. The matrix language constitutes the morphosyntactic framework for the constituents of both the matrix language and the embedded language. The matrix language and the embedded language are linked 1. to the principle of morpheme order and 2. to the principle of systemic morphemes:

> The Morpheme-Order Principle: In ML+EL constituents consisting of singly-occurring EL lexemes and any number of ML morphemes, surface morpheme order (reflecting surface syntactic relations) will be that of the ML. The System Morpheme Principle: all system morphemes which have a grammatical relations external to their head constituent (i.e. which participate in the sentence's thematic role grid) will from the ML. (Myers-Scotton 1993: 83)

The matrix language blocks the appearance of any morpheme from the embedded language that does not meet a certain congruence with the matrix language's counterpart.

> The MLF model limits the EL's main role to providing either content morphemes in mixed constituents or EL phrase-level constituents (EL islands), or both. (…) In bilingual speech, the structures of the Matrix Language (ML) are always preferred. Embedded Language (EL) islands (phrases from other varieties participating in the

> clause) are allowed if they meet EL well-formedness conditions, as well as those ML conditions applying to the clause as a whole (e.g. phrase placement). (Myers-Scotton and Jake 2009: 337)

The matrix language hypothesis assumes that syntactic morphemes (empty words or grammatical morphemes) from the embedded language are not inserted into the matrix language unless they appear in an Embedded Language Island. Morphemes with lexical content may be freely alternated, provided that the morphemes in question are congruent in some way with the existing counterpart in the matrix language. This principle applies to all situations, except where the switching is marked by the embedded language and the matrix language (dual morphology) and where the morphemes with lexical content of the embedded language are used in their bare form, without any marker from either language.

Code-switching and code-mixing are also present in Dongxiang, and, in some clauses, the Chinese elements are more numerous than the Dongxiang ones, and it is sometimes difficult to determine the nature of the phenomena. Below is an example where the Chinese elements are underlined:

(22)	'ajie	ajie	ire-wo!',	dajia	dou	huanying	gie-wo.
	elder.sister	elder.sister	come-PFV	everyone	all	everyone	do-PFV

'Everyone greeted her: Elder sister, elder sister, you're here!'

In this example, only one semantic element, *ire* 'come', and two grammatical elements (the perfective *wo* and the borrowed verb auxiliary *gie*) are of Dongxiang origin, while all the other elements in the sentence are of Chinese origin. This sentence is a mix between borrowings, with or without Dongxiang equivalents (*ajie* 'elder sister') and code-mixing, where Dongxiang equivalents exist. In this sentence, the equivalent for the Chinese element *dajia* (< *ʈA*^{42}*ʈɕiA*^{243} 大家 'everybody') is *ashigvala* (*ashigva* 'all' + *la* plural marker). However, the equivalent of the Chinese adverb *dou* (< *ʈu*^{243}都'all') in Dongxiang is another Chinese adverb, *igua* (< *i*^{243}*kuA*^{42}一挂 'all'), borrowed from Linxia Chinese. The verb *huanying gie* 'to welcome' (< *χuæ̃*^{243}*iŋ*^{243} 欢迎), is a Chinese borrowing, integrated with the auxiliary *gie* 'to do'. The other Dongxiang equivalent is *bayasilan jielie* litt.'happily receiving', where *jielie* is a Linxia borrowing (< *tɕie* 接 'receive' and lexical derivation suffix *-lie*). In the clause *dajia dou huanying gie* 'everybody welcomes (her)', *dajia dou* forms a single unit, as in Standard Chinese those two adverbs functions together (*dajia dou* 大家都, where *dajia* 'everybody' has to be followed by *dou* so the clause is grammatically correct). Therefore, we can identify different layers of mixture here: a first layer with integrated borrowings (*ajie, huanying gie*) and a second layer where Chinese integrated elements are replaced by Standard Chinese elements. The replacement in the code-switching context seems to operate on the same adverbial and nominal elements that were initially borrowed from Linxia Chinese, while the verbal elements remain Dongxiang.

Some other ambiguous situations include the use of classifiers with Chinese numerals. Usually, Dongxiang numbers from 1 to 10 are of Mongolic origin, while all numbers above are borrowed from Chinese, for example, *nie* < Mmon *niGe* 'one'; *ghua* < Mmon *qoyar* 'two'; *dolong* < Mmon *dulan* 'seven', *ershi* < LX *er*^{42}*ʂʅer*^{42} (二十) 'twenty'; *sishiba* < LX *sɿ*^{42}*ʂʅpA*^{243} (四十八) 'forty-eight', etc.

When the classifier is used together with Chinese numeral (where a Dongxiang numeral exists) and a borrowed noun, it is quite visible that all the items are borrowed together, as a single unit. Those clauses are clearly identifiable as code-mixing, for example:

(23) beifu gie-se haoxiang <u>liang zuo dashan</u>-ni beilie-gva-zhuo gie-se.
carry say-CSL look.like two CL mountains-ACC carry -CAUS-PROG say-PST
'He was carrying something on the back as if there were two mountains'

In this example, Chinese *liang* 'two' could be replaced by Dongxiang numeral *ghua*, and Chinese *dashan* 'mountain' by Dongxiang *ula*. The adverb preceding the sequence *haoxiang* 'look like' is also of Chinese origin, but has a post-nominal Dongxiang equivalent *mutu* 'as'. The segment *liang zuo dashan* is integrated in the sentence with the Dongxiang accusative suffix *-ni*.

When the numeral does not have any Dongxiang equivalent, it is sometimes difficult to interpret whether the classifier is borrowed together with the numeral or not:

(24) ene kun nie udu <u>jiushijiu</u> <u>gie</u> bari-wo ma!
DEM man one day ninety-nine CL catch-PFV MP
'He caught ninety-nine ones in one day.' (Field, 1997:313)

In this sentence, *gie* is borrowed from the general Linxia classifier *ge* 个, but is not followed by a noun, Rather, it serves as a reference to a subject and forms part of an anaphora.

Among the recent developments in the Dongxiang language, it is noteworthy to mention the use of several direct loans and calques from Standard Chinese. Those are particles (1) de_1 (< *de* 的) as a genitive, subordinate clauses and relative clause marker; (2) de_2 (< *de* 地) manner adverbial and (3) de_3 (< *de* 得) degree and potential marker. Giving the significant number of loans in the Dongxiang language, the degree of integration of these elements in Dongxiang is difficult to gauge. It is sometimes not clear whether those items form part of intra-phrasal code-switching or if they are just embedded elements within a highly sinicised environment.

6.6.1 Genitive, subordinate clause and relative clause marker *de/ji* (< 的)

As we have seen, most adjectives are borrowed from Linxia Chinese together with the marker *-ji* 的. However, some others bear the suffix *-ni*, which is also the form for the indigenous genitive marker and the third-person possession marker in Dongxiang. As in Linxia the adjective marker *ji* 的 is formally identical to the genitive marker, the two particles' functions have merged under the same form in Dongxiang. Therefore, when combined with adjectives, *-ni* can be used as a calque, integrating the other functions of the Chinese marker *ji* 的:

(25)	Enedu	jiu	zhengienni	saigvan	oqin	wo
	today	so	really	beautiful	girl	COP

‘Today, there was a very beautiful girl’

The use of Dongxiang's adjective marker *-ni* is a lot more limited than in Standard Chinese as it can be only combined with adjectives of Chinese origin. Both marker *-ji* and *-ni* are originally based on Linxia marker *ji* 的, but are the result of two different mechanisms. *-ji* is a direct borrowing which has partially preserved its original functions, and *-ni* is a calque. Those two markers are attested in earlier sources (Buhe 1986; Field 1997) and should be identified as borrowed adjectives markers.

As well as being a marker for relative subordinates, the genitive and the accusative, the Dongxiang marker *-ni* can be used to nominalise adjectives:

(26) youshi-de bi musi chighan-ni musi-zhuo, youshi-de
sometimes-DAT 1 wear white-NMLZ wear-PROG sometimes-LOC
khara-ni musi-zhuo.
black-NMLZ wear-PROG
'Sometimes, I wear white, sometimes black (clothes).'

In Standard Chinese as well as in Linxia, the particle *ji* or *de* 的 can also have the same de-adjectival function:

(27) 菊花开了，有红的,有黄的. (XDHYCD 2016:272)
jú huā kāi le, yǒu hóng-de, yǒu huáng-de
chrysanthemums open PFV have red-SUBS have yellow SUBS
'The Chrysanthemums have bloomed, some red, some yellow.'

In addition, this de-adjectival marker is also attested under the form *de* 的, that is, the phonetic counterpart of Linxia's particle *ji* 的 in Northern varieties and Standard Chinese. Most of the adjectives combined with the particle *de* are of Chinese origin (e.g. *canjide* < *cánjí de* 残疾的 'handicaped'; *ganjinde* < *gānjìng de* 干净的 'clean'; *dadade* < *dàdà de* 大大的 'very big', etc.). Therefore, is should be identified as part of an inseparable unit, as it is the case when the marker *-ji* is borrowed together with the adjectives. Again, the Standard Chinese form is replacing a particle borrowed from Linxia Chinese. Therefore, it's a formal replacement of a borrowing. The marker *de* 的 can also be combined with adjectives of Dongxiang origin:

(28) ingiese jiu agvui-de ingie gie-ne.
then so large-DE like.this say-IPFV
'Then it becomes large like this'

In this particular case, the adjective is of Dongxiang origin, and the particle *de* is a direct borrowing of the Standard Chinese particle *de* 的, a function that is usually borne by the indigenous Dongxiang form *-ni*. Therefore, this is a calque of an existing syntactic element, replaced by its Chinese counterpart.

In addition, the particle *de* 的 can be clause final in Standard Chinese, used as a relative proposition marker:

(29) 他昨天来的.
tā zuótiān lái de
3 yesterday come DE
'He came yesterday.' (Li and Thompson, 1989:588)

The marker *de* can also be used in the same manner in Dongxiang:

(30) ingie ulie ire-ne, gie-zhuo de.
then NEG come-IPFV say-PROG DE
'Then he said he was not going to come.'

In this particular case, *de* is a direct borrowing, copying the Standard Chinese clause final particle *de* used as in example 29).

In this kind of clause, the element immediately preceding the particle *de* has no equivalent in Dongxiang, and is used as a modal particle to put emphasis on a certain part of the clause and should be identified as code-mixing.

Sometimes the Standard Chinese particle *de* 的 is also used in the Dongxiang language as a genitive marker, in place of the indigenous form *-ni*, but only when it is associated with a Chinese borrowing that precedes or follows it. In other words, it is part of a fixed segment inserted as such in a sentence, a phenomenon that can be identified as code-switching (see Auer 1999; Myers-Scotton 1993):

(31) baer olon de shuzi wo.
money lot DE number COP
'It's a lot of money'

In this example, the word of Chinese origin, *shuzi* 'number' (< *ʂu*^{42}*ʈsʅ* 数字) which follows the Chinese particle *de*, prompts the speaker to use is. The whole expression it is a calque of the Linxia Chinese expression *ʈuə*^{243}*ji ʂu*^{42} *ʈsʅ* 多的数字 (lit. 'a big number') in which part of the elements is a direct borrowing. The SOV word order is preserved. The subject (*baer* 'money') and predicate (*wo* COP) elements are Dongxiang, therefore the matrix language is Dongxiang, while the segment *de shuzi* is the embedded Chinese element.

In other cases, the incorporated element is an entire expression, borrowed and inserted into the sentence. The word order is retained, the matrix language remains Dongxiang, and the phenomenon is one of intra-phrasal code-switching:

(32) matu gie-se ede [fanzhen-de-hua], gaokao gie-se munao ma!
how do-QUOT now anyway baccalaureate say-CSL boring MP
'Anyway, now talking about the baccalaureate is boring'

Finally, in other cases, the inserted segment is completely Chinese, but the word order does no longer conforms to Dongxiang's; the matrix language is therefore Chinese:

(33) hhe shi [man bu keneng de shiqing]
DEM COP all NEG possible GEN thing
'That is completely impossible'

We see that when the marker *de* 的 is used as a genitive in the Dongxiang language, it always forms part of a Chinese segment. This shows us that, although Chinese-Dongxiang code-switching phenomena are not new (Bao 2006), the varieties used during the process are now different. In all the occurrences we have recorded, the Chinese marker is found as in Standard Chinese and the North-western Mandarin dialects *de* 的, and not as in Linxia *tɕi* or *tɕ'i*.

6.6.2 Manner adverbial *de/ji* (< 地)

As explained above, manner adverbial *-ji* in Dongxiang is a borrowing from Linxia Chinese that is used with adjectives. Sometimes, this manner adverbial is also found in Dongxiang as *-de*, which is the Standard Chinese or North-western Mandarin form of the same manner adverbial:

(34) giedon tongxue-la yizhong-de bai-zhuo, jijizhazha-de
some classmate-PL everywhere-LOC be-PROG chirping-MAN

zhishouhuajiao gie-zhuo.
gesticulate BVA-PROG
'A few of my classmates have gathered and are waving their hands at Keliya.'

Here, the manner adverbial *de* here is a direct borrowing from the Standard Chinese particle *de* 地, which shows that Dongxiang source of borrowings is no longer exclusively limited to Linxia. This form is completely absent in previous sources (Buhe 1987; Field 1997). Moreover, in the descriptions of these authors, the adjective in the construction was always of Chinese origin and had to be duplicated, which is not the case in our corpus, where adjectives of Dongxiang origin can also be used without being duplicated. Furthermore, in the initial constructions with the manner adverbial borrowed from Linxia, no other element could be inserted between the adjective and the verb. However, when the manner adverbial appears as *de*, a numeral or other elements can be inserted in between, for example:

(35) ingiese ene laowa niedun-de nie bangmang gie-ne.
then DEM raven speedy-MAN one help BVA-IPFV
'The raven hastened to help him'

In the latter example, *bangmang gie* is the verbal compound borrowed from Chinese *bangmang* 帮忙 (it could be a borrowing from Chinese, Linxia or North-western Mandarin as they all have the same form). It is code-mixing where the Chinese expression *bāng yī gè máng* 帮一个忙 (help-one-task) 'to help' is copied and mixed, with the integrated borrowed auxiliary *gie*. The intermediate element *nie* 'one' between the adjective and the verbal compound is not syntactically necessary, but does not affect the word order. In Standard Chinese, it is sometimes possible to insert a complement between the adjective bearing the manner adverbial and the verb.

6.6.3 Particle *de* (< *de* 得) as a potential marker

In Chinese, when *dé* 得 is a verb, it bears the second tone, and means 'to obtain', 'to suit', 'to satisfy', 'to finish', 'to be able to', etc. When *de* 得 is a particle, it is realised with a neutral tone and introduce a complement of the degree. In that case, it follows the verb and precedes the complement expressing the degree, which can be expressed using an adjective or an adjectival compound:

(36) 写得非常好. (XDHYCD 2016:273)
xiě dé fēicháng hǎo
write DEG extremely well
'(It's) very well written.'

It can also introduce a complement of potentiality and is then followed by another verb or a compound verb:

(37) 拿得动. (XDHYCD 2016:273)
ná de dòng
take POT move
'(something) moveable .'

In Linxia Chinese, degree and potentiality are expressed using a particle different from that found in Standard Chinese, which is *tʂe* 者 (着). It functions in the same manner as *de* 得 in Standard Chinese:

(38) 尕丫头干散者尺码没. (LXFY 1996:208-209)
kA^{43}yA^{243}tou^{243} gæ̃^{243}sæ̃^{43} tʂe tʂ'i^{43}mA^{43} miei
young.girl beautiful DEG describe NEG
'The girl is so beautiful (to the point that) she cannot even be described.' (姑娘漂亮得没法儿形容).

In Dongxiang, the verb *olu-* 'to obtain' is used with other verbs to introduce a complement of potentiality, in the same manner the Chinese particle *de* 得 in Standard Chinese and *tʂe* 者 in Linxia are in [V *de* V] constructions:

(39) ene kien ye khati kielie-zhi <u>olu</u> shida-ne!
DEM who also Chinese say-SIM obtain can-IPFV
'I know another one who can speak Chinese!'

In this example, the verb *olu-* 'obtain' can be omitted and the auxiliary *shida* 'can' can be used on its own. In Modern Mongolian, potentiality is expressed by the auxiliary verb *čadax* (чадах ᠴᠢᠳᠠᠬᠤ) 'can', used immediately after a verb to express the ability or the capacity to do something, and no other element can be inserted between the two verbs. This verb is attested in Middle Mongol (40) as well as in modern Chakhar (41) and corresponds to the Dongxiang verb *shida*:

(40) ken üile-dün čida-qu. (HYYY section IIa 5v4)
who do-NMLZ can-INF
'Who could have done this?

(41) ᠡᠨᠡ ᠠᠵᠢᠯ ᠢ ᠪᠢ ᠪᠡᠶᠡᠯᠡᠭᠦᠯᠵᠦ ᠴᠢᠳᠠᠨ᠎ᠠ᠃ (Chinggeltei 1991:360)
Энэ ажлыг би биелүүлж чадна
Ene ajil-ig bi biyelüül-ž čad-na
DEM work-ACC do-GRD provide-IPFV
'I can finish this work.'

In example (39), the construction *kielie olu shida* copies the Chinese construction *shūo de liǎo* 说得了 'to be able to speak', attested in Standard Chinese. As we have seen, *de* 得 has several grammatical values in Standard Chinese, and in this example, *olu* has more or less the same function as the particle *de* 得 when it is used to introduce a potential complement. Since the Chinese homonymous verb *dé* 得 means 'to obtain' like the Dongxiang verb *olu*, there seems to have been an amalgam between the meanings and functions of the Dongxiang counterpart. More precisely, as the verb *olu* shares some of the semantic values of the Chinese verb *dé* 得, *olu* has expanded its own functions and adopted those of the particle *dé* 得 when expressing potentiality.

In the following example, the verb *olu* is used to introduce a complement of degree:

(42) shoushu gie-se otu olu-zhi agi da-ne.
operation do-COND hurt obtain-SIM give cannot-IPFV
'The operation is so painful, it cannot be done' (painful to the point that it cannot)

In this example, the verb *olu-* is not essential and can be omitted in the construction. It clearly introduces the complement of degree of the action *shoushu gie* 'to do an operation', which is expressed by the verbal compound that follows it *agi dane* 'not to be able to do'. It could be a copy of the Chinese expression *téng de gěi bù liǎo* 疼得给不了 'painful to the point that it cannot be done'. This is a construction completely absent in Mongolic languages. The verb *olu* has therefore become somewhat grammaticalised, but has retained its original verbal function. It can be considered as code-mixing (rather than code-swicthing) as the verb *olu* is of Mongolic origin, and is suffixed with the simultaneity converb *-zhi*, thus syntactically integrated in the Dongxiang language.

In addition, the particle *de* is also used as a direct loan with similar functions:

(43) Nanxin-de-ji, mati gie-se jiu yinggaiji maimai gie-zho.
poor-DEG-much how do-QUOT so must business BVA-PROG
'We were very poor, so we thought we should go do business'

(44) bijien ene huang kao-de-dao-de be, matu gie-se gie man be
1PL DEM year take.exam-POT-RES-DE MP how do-PST do all MP
'I don't know if I can pass the exam this year, but I've done it all.'

In example (44), *nanxin-de-ji* is a calque of the expression *qióng de jí* 穷得极 (poor-DEG-extreme), where the element *ji* 'extreme' is a direct borrowing from Standard Chinese, and *nanxin* an integrated borrowing from Linxia. In example (44), it is a spontaneous borrowing of the expression *kǎo de dào* 考得到 (pass.an.exam POT reach), which is borrowed as a whole.

When the particle *de* is a direct borrowing used to introduce potentiality and degree complements, it is always part of an entirely Chinese segment. This shows that it is borrowed as an integral expression, inserted into the sentence in Dongxiang, and is an Embedded Language Island.

6.6.4 Discussion

We have seen that de_1 (< *de* 的), de_2 (< *de* 地) and de_3 (< *de* 得) have different functions and appear in different contexts through diverse mechanisms in the Dongxiang language:

1. de_1 (< *de* 的) is attested:
   - As a direct borrowing (under the form *-ji*) and a calque (under the form *-ni*) of Linxia Chinese and used as a derivational suffix with borrowed adjectives;

- As a direct borrowing from Standard/North-western Chinese (under the form *de*) and used as a derivational suffix with borrowed adjectives;
- As a direct borrowing from Standard/North-western Chinese (under the form *de*) and used as a syntactic marker for relative clauses;
- As a direct borrowing from Standard/North-western Chinese (under the form *-de*) and used as a genitive marker;

2. de_2 (< *de* 地) is attested:
   - As a direct borrowing from Linxia (under the form *-jï*) used with adjectives as a manner adverbial;
   - As a direct borrowing from from Standard/North-western Chinese (under the form *de*) used with adjectives as a manner adverbial;

3. de_3 (< *de* 得) is attested:
   - As a calque (under the form *olu*) to introduce a potential complement;
   - As a direct borrowing from Standard/North-western Chinese (under the form *-de*) to introduce a degree complement;
   - As a direct borrowing *-de* to introduce a potential complement;

These calques and borrowings are not equally integrated and therefore do not form part of a same phenomenon. They can be identified as part of code-switching, code-mixing or as grammatical borrowings in the process of 'being stabilised'.

The particles calqued and borrowed from Linxia seem to be earlier developments, while those from North-western Chinese dialects and Standard Chinese seem to have appeared fairly recently. The degree of integration of the Chinese particles therefore, varies according to their source. The meanings and functions of the suffix *-jï* have developed so to express manner, following the example of Linxia *tɕi* 地, and then adopted the meanings and functions of the Dongxiang suffix *-ni* to mark adjectives of Chinese origin. Those two suffixes have further developed and have fully grammaticalised, as they can be used with all kinds of adjectives and no longer form a single unit with the adjective they are borrowed with. Therefore, a new adjective suffix category is developing in Dongxiang. The development process is not as simple as it is for direct loans: calques are always based on existing structures and functions found in Dongxiang. This is the case for the borrowed adjective marker *-jï* which was first borrowed as a direct loan, then calqued with the indigenous marker *-ni*. Dongxiang has then calqued again different functions of the Linxia manner adverbial *ʨi* 地 using the Dongxiang suffix *-jï*. Therefore, it's a calque of a calque. In the same manner, the verb *olu* has first been associated with the Chinese verb *dé* 得 because they shared some semantic values. Later, it has further calqued the functions of the particle *de* 得 by using the verb *olu* to introduce degree and potential complements.

When used as direct loans, the Chinese marker *de* 的 is used as genitive and the marker *de* 得 is used to introduce degree and potential complements always form parts of a borrowed segment of a clause. It is then easily identifiable as code-switching, and more specifically, as an intra-clause code-switching where Dongxiang is the matrix language and Chinese the embedded one. This also complies with the empty-words constraint as defined above. However, the adjective marker de_1 (< *de* 的), and the manner adverbial de_2 (< *de* 地) are a lot more independent and are not always used in a borrowed segment or an embedded language island. The two direct loans function like their indigenous counterpart *-jï* et *-ni*, calqued from Chinese. Moreover, those suffixes do not constraint the Dongxiang language word order as they used after the adjective, like any Dongxiang suffix. They are a reinterpretation of the forms borrowed from Standard Chinese, an alternative to the Mongolic and Linxia suffixes.

Finally, regarding the Chinese borrowed adjective markers *-jï* and *-ni*, as well as the marker *de* (< *de* 的) used to mark relative clauses, there are no equivalent Dongxiang suffix or particles with the same functions which could have been replaced by their Chinese counterpart. Therefore, they should be identified as grammatical borrowings, but not necessarily integrated ones. In all cases where they appear, the matrix language is clearly Dongxiang. The position of the marker *de* used at the end of a sentence and after a verb itself bearing a finite marker conflicts with the word order and the syntax. In fact, only an unmarked imperative or infinitive verb or a verb suffixed with a non-finite marker can, in principle, be at the end of a sentence. Furthermore, non-finite or finite markers are not cumulative, so this marker cannot be considered a suffix and is, in fact, a non-modal final particle. This contradicts the MLF, where the word order of the Matrix language should not be affected. Furthermore. The Matrix language hypothesis assumes that syntactic morphemes from the embedded language appear in an embedded language island, while lexical morphemes can alternate freely if they appear with their matrix language counterpart. This is the case when the borrowed Chinese marker *de* expresses the genitive in Dongxiang in place of the indigenous marker *-ni* and forms part of a borrowed segment, a single unit, which can be identified as an embedded language island.

Then, how should the syntactic morphemes be identified when the functional morphemes of the embedded language are not blocked? Myers-Scotton attempts to answer this question by proposing to identify the other functional morphemes with semantic content morphemes. For example, some prepositions are systemic morphemes and others are lexical content morphemes[109]. The blocking hypothesis predicts that this preposition can be alternated if it satisfies the congruence condition. The marker *de* used to mark relative clauses never appears in an embedded language island, and it does not relate to a semantic element, since it is highly grammaticalised, both in Chinese and Dongxiang. It therefore does not fit into the matrix language hypothesis as defined by Myers-Scotton. On the other hand, it can be identified as an emphasis marker[110], as found in Chinese, where, although it is highly grammaticalised, its lexical value has not completely disappeared.

To conclude, the Dongxiang language is in a situation of change, part of an 'switching-mixing-borrowing' continuum in the midst of a 'mixing-borrowing' transition. In the current situation, the use of certain elements, such as the adjective and relative clauses marker de_1 (< *de* 的) and the manner adverbial de_2 (< *de* 地), is quite frequently used. This suggests that these grammatical

109 In English, some locative or temporal prepositions are systemic morphemes because they have the characteristic [+ quantity] However, prepositions such as *of*, in *I don't approve of John*, are lexical morphemes because they can be assigned a thematic role.

110 Categorised in Chinese as *yǔqìcí* 语气词 'modal particles'.

elements will stabilise and become systematic, thus integrated. On the other hand, the use of other direct borrowings, such as that the genitive marker de_1 (< *de* 的) and particle de_3 (< *de* 得) to introduce degree and potential complements, seems to be marginal for the time being and is clearly still identifiable as code-mixing.

Conclusion

The identity of the Dongxiang community's members is guided by a strong sentiment of religious unity. The Dongxiang language only emerged as a constituent element of Dongxiang identity, in terms of its contrast to other communities, after the establishment of their national minority status. Today, the 'Dongxiang' identity, as an ethnic construct, is widespread throughout the community.

The main languages within the Dongxiang linguistic community can be divided into the languages of communication, which are Dongxiang (vernacular), Linxia and the northern dialects associated with Putonghua (vehicular), and the written language with a religious function, namely Arabic. Today, this community comprises monolinguals (Dongxiang), bilinguals (Dongxiang-Linxia) and trilinguals (Dongxiang-Linxia-Putonghua/Beifanghua Dialects), who together form a heterogeneous group of speakers. Plurilingualism varies in accordance with a speaker's place of residence, sex and level of education. It would therefore be difficult to establish a single, representative profile of all the speakers within the community. We can say, however, that the Dongxiang community is predominantly bilingual.

Existing models of macro-sociolinguistic description, whether specific to the Chinese context (T'sou 1988) or offering a more global description of societies (de Swaan 1993), shed light from a perspective external to the community on the relationships between the languages of communication present in the linguistic galaxy of which Dongxiang is a part. Here, Putonghua represents the hyper-central language; the various northern dialects, the central languages; Linxia, a peripheral language and Dongxiang, a hyper-peripheral language. However, these models do not allow for the fact that speakers do not recognise Putonghua, Northern dialect and Linxia as being distinct varieties. Nor do they allow for the inclusion of Arabic, which plays a very important role in the community from a representational perspective, without actually having a communicative function as such. This issue prompted us to analyse the domains in which the languages are used, a process that allowed us to integrate of all the languages present in the linguistic landscape and to define, to a certain degree, their functions. Dongxiang and the Chinese languages do not appear to be in opposition, either in terms of function (they can be functionally interchangeable) or of representation (one language is not denigrated in favour of another). There exists a perfect bilingualism in which the functions of Linxia and Dongxiang are shared across virtually all domains in which either language is used. From the perspective of linguistic representations, the vast majority of speakers struggle to identify and differentiate between the varieties of Chinese (Linxia, Putonghua and Northern varieties), which makes it impossible to establish a hierarchy for the Chinese languages or to identify potential linguistic insecurity. Nonetheless, most speakers do recognise that there exist both a standardised variety and informal dialects of Chinese. This leads me to conclude that the Dongxiang linguistic community is in a state of unconscious diglossia, that is, there is a de facto hierarchy of languages, but it is not recognised by speakers and is not expressed in the form of a general feeling of linguistic insecurity within the community.

Although the number of Chinese speakers (all varieties) far exceeds that of Dongxiang speakers, and while bilinguals and trilinguals are increasingly commonplace, the number of native Dongxiang speakers remains stable. Moreover, neither representations nor linguistic practices suggest that Dongxiang is threatened with imminent abandonment in favour of a more prestigious variety.

Through contacts and bilingualism, the Dongxiang language has been influenced by Linxia Chinese at the phonological, lexical, and morphosyntatic levels, developing new syntactic categories such as classifiers and manner adverbials. However, it still remains strictly *Mongolic* and a highly suffixal language. With the increasing influence of Standard Chinese, new elements are being introduced in the Dongxiang's people speech during the code-switching and code-mixing process. Interestingly, the grammatical elements being replaced by the Standard Chinese forms are, very often, originally borrowings from Linxia. This shows the consistency of the categories being influenced as well as the different layers of Chinese influence that can be found in the Dongxiang language. It also shows how Chinese regional dialects are being affected by the progressive shift to Standard Chinese.

Bibliography

Arends, Jacques, Myusken Pieter and Smith Norval (eds) (1995). *Pidgins and Creoles An Introduction*. Amsterdam: John Benjamins.

Auer, Peter (1999). 'From Code-Switching via Language Mixing to Fused Lects: Towards a Dynamic Typology of Bilingual Speech', *International Journal of Bilingualism*, 3 (4), 309–332.

Bao, Saren 包萨仁 (2006). *Ménggŭ yŭzú dōngxiāng yŭ yŭ hànyŭ de jiēchù yánjiū* 蒙古语族东乡语与汉语的接触研究 [A study of the contact between Dongxiang and Chinese]. PhD dissertation. Beijing: Peking University.

Bao, Saren 包萨仁 (2017). *Dōngxiāng yŭ hànyŭ jiēchù yánjiū* 东乡语汉语接触研究 [A study of contact between Dongxiang and Chinese languages]. Beijing: China International Radio Press.

Bao, Lianqun 包聯群 (2011). 言語接触と言語変異ー中国黒龍江省ドルブットモンゴル族コミュニティー言語を事例としてー [Language contact and language variation: the case of the Dörbed Mongolian community language in Heilongjiang Province, China]. Tokyo: Gendai Tosho.

Bo, Gujin 博古今 et al. (2008). *Xiàndài hànyŭ cídiăn* 现代汉语词典 [A dictionary of contemporary Chinese]. Huhehaote: Neimenggu daxue chubanshe.

Brosig, Benjamin (2015). 'Negation in Mongolic', *Journal de la Société Finno-Ougrienne*, 95, 67–136.

Buhe 布和 (Böke) (1985). 'Diingsiyang kelen-ii qamar-un geyigiiliigci n kiged ng-iin tuqai' [The nasal consonants *n* and *ng* in Dongxiang], *OMYSS* (2), 1–6.

Buhe 布和 (Böke) (1986). *Dōngxiāng yǔ hé ménggǔ yǔ* 东乡语和蒙古语 [Dongxiang and Mongolian], Huhehaote: Neimenggu chubanshe.

Buhe 布和 (Böke) (1987). *Dōngxiāng yǔ huàyǔ cáiliào* 东乡语话语材料 [Dongxiang language material]. Huhehaote: Neimenggu daxue chubanshe.

Bulot, Thierry and Blanchet, Philippe (2011). *Dynamiques de la langue française au 21ème siècle: une introduction à la sociolinguistique* (consulted on 14/03/2016). Rennes: Université Rennes 2 <http://www.sociolinguistique.fr/cours-4-4.html>.

Cai, Rang 才让 (2007). *Tǔbō shǐ gǎo* 吐蕃史稿 [A Draft History of the Tubo Kingdom]. Lanzhou: Gansu Renmin Chubanshe.

Cao, Guangshun 曹广顺, Redouane Djamouri and Alain Peyraube (eds) (2015). *Languages in Contact in North China, Historical and Synchronic Studies*. Paris: Collection des cahiers de linguistique Asie Orientale.

Calvet, Louis-Jean (1998). 'Insécurité Linguistique et Représentations. Approche Historique'. In Calvet Louis-Jean and Moreau M.-L (eds), *Une ou des normes? Insécurité linguistique et normes endogènes en Afrique francophone*, pp. 9–17. Paris: Didier Erudition (coll. Langues et développement).

Chen, Qinbing 陈其斌 (2006). *Dōngxiāng shèhuì yánjiū* 东乡社会研究 [A study on the Dongxiang society]. PhD dissertation. Beijing: Peking University.

Chen, Naixiong 陈乃雄 (1987). *Bǎo'ān yǔ hé ménggǔ yǔ* 保安语和蒙古语 [The Bonan and the Mongolian language]. Huhehaote: neimenggu renmin chubanshe.

de Crespigny, Rafe (1984). *Northern Frontiers: The Policies and Strategy of the Later Han Empire*. Canberra: Australian National University Press.

de Rascheziltz, Igor (2004). *The Secret History of the Mongols*. Leiden, Boston: Brill.

de Swaan, Abram (1993). 'The Emerging World Language System, Introduction', *International Political Science Review, (special issue on the Political Sociology of Language Conflict, editor AdS)*, 14 (3), 219–226.

DeGraff, Michel (2002). 'Relexification: A Reevaluation', *Linguistic Anthropology*, 44 (4), 321–414.

Delige'erma, and Bo, Sude (2006). *Ménggǔ yǔzú yǔyán gàilùn* 蒙古语族语言概论 [An introduction to Mongolic languages]. Beijing: Zhongyang minzu daxue chubanshe.

Djamouri, Redouane (2015). 'Object Positioning in Tangwang'. In Cao, Djamouri, and Peyraube (eds), *Languages in Contact in North China, Historical and Synchronic Studies*, pp. 251–276. Paris: Collection des cahiers de linguistique Asie Orientale (13).

Dunnell, Ruth (2014). 'The Anxi Principality: [un]Making a Muslim Mongol Prince in Northwest China during the Yuan Dynasty', *Central Asiatic Journal – Special Tangut Edition*, 57, 185–200.

Dwyer, Arienne (1992). 'Altaic Elements in the Línxia Dialect [of NW Chinese]: Contact-induced Change on the Yellow River Plateau', *Journal of Chinese Linguistics*, 20 (1), 160–79.

Erdal, Marcel (2004). *A Grammar of Old Turkic.* Leiden: Brill.

Fergusson, Charles (1959). 'Diglossia', *Word*, 15, 325–340.

Field, Kenneth (1991). 'Hui Loanwords in Dongxiang Mongolian'. In *Proceedings of the Seventeenth Annual Meeting of the Berkeley Linguistics Society: General Session and Parasession on The Grammar of Event Structure*, 92–106.

Field, Kenneth (1997). *A Grammatical Overview of Santa Mongolian*. PhD Dissertation. Santa Barbara: University of California.

Fishman, Joshua, (1967). 'Bilingualism with and without Diglossia, Diglossia with and without Bilingualism', *Journal of Social Issues*, 32.

—— (1968). *Readings in the Sociology of Language*. The Hague, Paris: Mouton.

—— (1971). *Sociolinguistique*. Paris: Nathan.

—— (1986). 'Domains and the Relationship between Micro and Macrosociolinguistics'. In J. J. Gumperz, and D. Hymes (eds), *Directions in Sociolinguistics: The Ethnography of Communication*, pp. 435–453. Oxford: Blackwell,.

Fried, Robert Wayne (2010). *A Grammar of Bao'an Tu, a Mongoic Language of Northwest China.* PhD Dissertation. Buffalo: University of Buffalo.

Fuller, Medina N. (2020). 'How Bilingual Verbs are Built: Evidence from Belizean Varieties of Contact Spanish', *Canadian Journal of Linguistics/ Revue canadienne de linguistique*, 65(1), 122–132.

Giles, H., Bourhis, RY, and Taylor, DM (1977). 'Towards a Theory of Language in Ethnic Group Relations'. In Giles, H. (ed.), *Language, Ethnicity, and Intergroup Relations.* New York: Academic Press.

Goldman, Merle (1986). 'Religion in Post-Mao China', *The Annals of the American Academy of Political and Social Science*, 483, 146–156.

Georg, Stefan (2003). 'Mongghul', In Janhunen, Juha (ed.), *The Mongolic Languages*, pp. 268–306 London, New Yok: Routledge Language Family.

Grey, Alexandra (forthcoming 2025). 'Common Collateral: China's Official Common Language Gains Further Strength Against Minority Languages', *Melbourne Asia Review.*

Grossberg, Lawrence (1993). 'Cultural Studies and New Worlds.' In C. McCarthy, and W. Crichlow (eds), *Race, Identity and Representation*. New York: Routledge.

Grousset, René (1939). *L'empire des Steppes: Attila, Gengis Khan, Tamerlan.* Paris: Payot.

—— (1944). *Le conquérant du monde (Vie de Gengis-khan).* Paris: Albin Michel.

Gruntov, Ilya, and Mazo, Olga (2019). 'Mongghul, Mangghuer and Beyond: Estimating the Proximity', Вопросы языкового родства [*Journal of Language Relationship*], 17(3), 210–232.

Gumilev L. N (1998, reed. 2004). *Istoriia naroda khunnu* История народа хунну [History of the Hunnu people]. Moscow: AST.

Hangin, John G. (1973). *Köke Sudur (The blue chronicle): A Study of the First Mongolian Historical Novel by Injannasi.* Wiesbaden: Harrassowitz Verlag.

Hu, Zhaoyi 胡兆义 (2012). 'Zhōngguó xīběi mínzú dìqū nóngcūn pínkùn wèntí yánjiū—yǐ gānsù shěng dōngxiāng zú zìzhìxiàn wéi lì' 中国西北民族地区农村贫困问题研究—以甘肃省东乡族自治县为例 [A study of rural poverty in ethnic minority areas of northwestern China: A case study of Dongxiang Autonomous County in Gansu Province], *Níngxià dàxué xuébào (rénwén shèhuì kēxué bǎn)*, 5, 13–18.

Huang, Xing 黄行 (2000). *Zhōngguó shào shù mínzú yǔyán huólì yánjiū* 中国少数民族语言活力研究 [A study of the vitality of minority languages in China]. Beijing: Zhongguo Minzu daxue chuban she.

Israeli, Raphael (2002). *Islam in China*. Lanham: Lexington Books.

Janhunen, Juha (2003a). *The Mongolic Languages*. London, New York: Routledge Language Family.

—— (2003b). 'Shirongol and Shirongolic', *Studia Etymologica Cracoviensia*, 8, 83–89.

—— (2006). 'Sinitic and Non-Sinitic Phonology in the Languages of Amdo Qinghai'. In Christoph Anderl, and Halvor, Eifring (eds), *Studies in Chinese Language and Culture. Festschrift in Honour of Christoph Harbsmeier on the Occasion of His 60th Birthday*, pp. 261–268. Oslo: Hermes Academic Publishing.

Kim, Stephan (2003). 'Santa'. In Janhunen, Juha (ed.), *The Mongolic Language*, pp. 346–363. New York: Routledge.

Labov, William (1964). 'The Phonological Correlates of Social Stratification', *American Anthropologist*, 66, 164–176.

—— (1966). *The Social Stratification of English in New York City*. Cambridge: Cambridge University Press.

Lattimore, Owen (2006). 'Introduction in to Schramm, Louis M. The Monguors of the Kansu–Tibetan Frontier, Part I: Their Origin, History and Social Organization'. *Transactions of the American Philosophical Society*, N. S. 44:1 [Philadelphia 1954]. [New edition edited by Charles Kevin Stuart], pp. 86–108. Xining: Plateau Publishers.

Lee-Smith, Mei W. (1996). 'The Hezhou language'. In Stephen A. Wunn, Peter Mütrlhüsler & Danell T. Tryon (eds), *Atlas of Languages of Intercultural Communication in the Pacific. Asia, and the Americas, II, 2 (Trends in Linguistics, Documentation, l3)*, pp. 865–873. Berlin: Mouton de Gruyter.

Lefort, Julie (2013). 'Développement économique, urbanisation et pratiques linguistiques des jeunes dans le district de Dongxiang' [Economic development, urbanisation and young people's language practices in Dongxiang' district]. In Tirvassen, R. (ed.), *Actes de la conférence internationale « Langage, jeunesse et urbanité »*. Mauritius Institute of Education, University of Mauritius, Réduit. Paris: L'harmattan.

Lefort, Julie (2015a). 'Language Contact in North-West Gansu: Chinese directional verbs structure calques in the Dongxiang Language'. In Cao Guangshun, Redouane Djamouri, Alain Peyraube (eds), *Languages in Contact in North China Historical and Synchronic Studies*, pp. 385–408 Paris: Collection des cahiers de linguistique Asie Orientale (13).

Lefort, Julie (2015b). 'Calquing, Structural Borrowing and Metatypy in the Dongxiang Language', *Cahiers de Linguistique Asie Orientale*, 44, 150–168.

Lefort, Julie (2017). 'Contact-induced Change in the Dongxiang Language: The Emerging Category of Classifier', *Cahiers de Linguistique Asie Orientale*, 46, 1–20.

Lefort, Julie (2020). 'On the Reflexive-possessive Markers in the Dongxiang Language', *Language and Linguistics*, 21(4), 581–600.

Lefort, Julie (2022). 'Contact de langues et changements linguistiques en dongxiang' [Language contact and linguistic change in Dongxiang Mongolian], *Cahiers de Linguistique Asie Orientale* (17).

Lefort, Julie (2023). *A Dongxiang-English Glossary* 东乡语英语对照(初稿) Dunxian Kielien Yingyu Kielie. Open Access on HAL archives [hal-04208786v2].

Lefort, Julie (2023). Dongxiang *Short Stories (with Gloss and Annotations)* Vol. 1: (Dunxian kielien 东乡语小故事 [illegible])'. Open access on hal archives [hal-04015834].

Legrand, Jacques (1997). *Parlons Mongol*. Paris: L'harmattan.

Li, Charles, and Thompson, Sandra (1989). *Mandarin Chinese: A Functional Reference Grammar.* Santa Barbara: University of California Press.

Li, Dingren 李定仁, and Fu, Anquan 付安权 (2002). 'Dōngxiāng zú xiǎoxuéshēng hànyǔ wén xuéxí kùnnán tiáo chá yánjiū' 东乡族小学生汉语文学习困难与教学对策研究 [A study of the difficulties of Dongxiang minority primary school students in learning Chinese and the teaching strategies to implement in response], *Xīběi shīdà xuébào (shèhuì kēxué bǎn)*, 39 (3), 90–95.

Li, Keyu 李克郁 (1983). 'Qiǎn xī dōngxiāng zú hé yùgù zú de mínzú míngchēng' 浅析东乡族和裕固族的民族名称 [A brief analysis of the ethnic names of the Dongxiang and Yugur peoples]. In Ma Yushan (ed.), *Qīnghǎi shěng mínzú xuéhuì xuéshù lùnwén xuǎnjí (dì èr jí)* 青海省民族学会学术论文选集(第二辑). Xining: Qinghai Sheng Minzu Xuehui.

Lipman, Jonathan Neaman (1998). *Familiar Strangers: A History of Muslims in Northwest China*. Hong Kong: Hong Kong University Press.

Liu Ling 刘伶 et al. Lánzhōu dàxué zhōngwén xì línxià diàochá yánjiū zǔ 兰州大学中文系临夏调查研究组 [Research group on the Linxia Dialect,

Department of Chinese Language, Lanzhou University] (1996). Linxia fangyan 临夏方言. Lanzhou: Lanzhou daxue chu ban she.

Liu, Lydia (2004). *The Clash of Empires: The Invention of China in Modern World Making*. Cambridge: Harvard University Press.

Liu, Mingyue, Feng, Xiaolong, Zhao, Yifu, and Qiu, Huanguang (2023). 'Impact of Poverty Alleviation through Relocation: From the Perspectives of Income and Multidimensional Poverty', *Journal of Rural Studies*, 99, 35–44. Open access version consulted on 29/11/2024. <https://www.sciencedirect.com/science/article/abs/pii/S0743016723000384#:~:text=Poverty%20alleviation%20through%20relocation%20(PAR)>.

Liu, Zhaoxiong 刘照雄 (1983). *Dōngxiāng yǔ jiǎn zhì* 东乡语简志, Beijing: Minzu chubanshe.

Ma, Guifen 马桂芬 and Zao Guojun 赵国军 (2005). *Gānsù dōngxiāng zú rénkǒu biànqiān, fēnbù jí tèdiǎn* 甘肃东乡族人口变迁、分布及特点 [Population changes, distribution and characteristics of the Dongxiang ethnic group in Gansu]. Lanzou: Xibei Renkou.

Ma, Guozhong 马国忠, and Chen, Yuanlong 陈元龙 (2001, reed. 2012). 'Dōngxiāng yǔ hànyǔ cídiǎn' 东乡语汉语词典 [A Dongxiang-Chinese dictionary]. Lanzhou: Gansu minzu chubanshe.

Ma, Guozhong 马国忠, and Ma, Zixiang 马自相 (1982). Guānyú dōngxiāng zú zú yuán wèntí 关于东乡族族源问题 [On the origin of the Dongxiang ethnic group], *Xibei minzu daxue xuebao*, 3.

Ma, Hucheng 马虎成 (1992). 'Sāěrtă: Yīgè céngjīng bèi hūlüè de mínzú míngchēng—yě tán sā ěr tă yǔ dōngxiāngzú zúyuán (xià)' 撒尔塔：一个曾经被忽略的民族名称—也谈撒尔塔与东乡族族源(下) [Sarta: an ethnic name that was once ignored – also on the origin of the Sarta and the Dongxiang (part 2)], *Xibei minzu yanjiu*, 2, 55–67.

Ma, Shujun 马树钧 (1988). 'Hézhōuhuà de yǔyīn tèdiǎn' 河州话的语音特点 [Phonetic characteristics of the Hezhou dialect], *Xibei minzu daxue xuebao*, 4.

Ma, Xueli (2008). *Dōngxiāng zú zìzhìxiàn gàikuàng* 东乡族自治县概况 [Overview of Dongxiang Autonomous County]. Beijing: Minzu chubanshe.

Ma, Yinian 马以念 (2006). *Dàshān li de nǚháizi–dōngxiāng zú nǚtóng jiàoyù diàochá jì* 大山里的女孩子– 东乡族女童教育调查记 [Girls from the

Mountains – Records of education surveys on Dongxiang girls], Beijing: Guangming ribao chubanshe.

Ma, Zhiyong 马志勇 (1983). '"Sāěrtǎ" yǔ dōngxiāngzú zúyuan' "撒尔塔"与东乡族族源 [The origin of the Sarta people and the Dongxiang nationality], *Xibei minzu xueyuan xuebao (zhéxué shèhuì kēxué bǎn)*, 1, 31–48.

Ma, Zhiyong (2004). 'Guānyú dōngxiāngzú zú yuán wèntí' 关于东乡族族源问题 [On the question of the origin of the dongxiang people], *Linxia zhou minzu minjian wenhua xilie zongshu* (临夏州民族民间文化系列总书). Lanzhou: Lanzhou daxue chubanshe.

Mo, Chao 莫超, and Zhang, Wenxuan 张文轩 (2009). *Lánzhōu huà cídiǎn* 兰州方言词典 [Lanzhou Dialect Dictionary]. Lanzhou: Zhongguo shehui kexue chubanshe.

Morgan, David (1986, reedition 2007). *The Mongols. The Peoples of Europe Series*. Malden: Blackwell Publishing.

Mostaert, Antoine, and De Smedt, A. (1933). *Le dialecte Moguor parlé au Kansu occidental, IIIème partie, Dictionnaire monguor-français.* Beijing: Publications de l'Université Catholique.

Muysken, Pieter (1981). 'Halfway between Quechua and Spanish: The Case for Relexification'. In Highfield, Arnold and Albert Valdman (eds), *Historicity and Variation in Creole Studies*, pp. 52–78. *Ann Arbor: Karoma*.

Muysken, Pieter (2000). *Bilingual Speech: A Typology of Code-Mixing.* Cambridge University Press.

Myers-Scotton, Carol (1993). *Social Motivations for Code-Switching: Evidence from Africa*, Oxford: Clarendon Press.

Nasunbayar, Borjigin (1961). *Diingsiyang kelen-ii temdeglegee* [Records of the Dongxiang language], *StMo 3/1-5: fasc. 3*. 53–106.

National Bureau of Statistics of the People's Republic of China, Sixth National Census 2010. Consulted on 20/07/2015. <http://www.stats.gov.cn/tjsj/tjgb/rkpcgb/qgrkpcgb/201104/t20110428_30327.html>.

Nugteren, Hans (2003). 'Shira Yugur'. In Janhunen, Juha (ed.). *The Mongolic Languages*, pp. 265–285. London, New York: Routledge Language Family.

Nugteren, Hans (2011). *Mongolic Phonology and the Qinghai-Gansu Languages*. Utrecht. Doctoral Thesis. Leiden University.

Pétard, Jean-Pierre (1999). 'Les savoirs en psychologie sociale: histoire, productions et usages in Psychologie sociale' [Knowledge in social psychology: history, production and uses in Social Psychology], *Psychologie Sociale*, Rosny, Bréal, 1, 15–68.

Petitjean, Cécile (2009). *Représentations linguistiques et plurlinguisme* [Linguistic representations and plurilinguism]. Université de Provence-Aix-Marseille I, Université de Neuchâtel.

Platt, John (1977). 'A Model for Polyglossia and Multilingualism (with Special Reference to Singapore and Malaysia)', *Language in Society*, 6 (03). 361–378.

Poppe, Nicholas (1955a). 'The Turkic Loan Words in Middle Mongolian', *Central Asiatic Journal*, I (1), 36–42.

Poppe, Nicholas (1955b). 'Introduction to Mongolian Comparative Studies'. *Mémoires de la Société finnoougrienne*, p. 110. Helsinki.

Qi, Guo Zheng 祁国正 (2004), Gānsù shěng dōngxiāng zú zìzhìxiàn shuāngyǔ jiàoxué shíyàn甘肃省东乡族自治县双语教学实验 [Bilingual teaching experiment in Dongxiang Autonomous County, Gansu Province], *Xibei Minzu yanjiu*, 4.

Rybatzki, Volker (2003). 'Intra-Mongolic Taxonomy'. In Janhunen, Juha (ed), *The Mongolic Languages*, pp. 364–390. London, New York: Routledge Language Family.

Schram, Louis M. J. (1957), reis. (2006). 'Introduction'. In Stuart, Kevin (ed.) *The Monguors of the Kansu-Tibetan Frontier I–III (Transactions of the American Philosophical Society, N. S. 44:1), New Series—Vol. 44*. Xining: Plateau Publications.

Sechenchogt (斯钦朝克图) (1999). *Kāngjiāyǔ yánjiū* 康家语研究 [A strudy on the Kangjia language]. Shanghai: Yuandong Chubanshe.

Slater, Keith (2003). *A Grammar of Mangghuer, a Mongolic language of China's Qinghai-Gansu Sprachbund.* London, New York: RoutledgeCurzon.

Statistical Bulletin on the Economic and Social Situation of Dongxiang Autonomous County (2011) Gansu Bureau of Statistics. Consulted on 10/08/2014. <http://www.gstj.gov.cn/www/HdClsContentDisp.asp?Id=27335>.

Stuart, Kevin (2006) (ed.). *The Monguors of the Kansu-Tibetan Frontier I-III (Transactions of the American Philosophical Society, N. S. 44:1). New Series—Vol. 44.* Xining: Plateau Publications.

Svantesson, Jan-olof et al. (2005). *The Phonology of Mongolian*. Oxford: Oxford University Press.

Thomason, Sarah Grey (2001). *Language Contact.* Edinburgh: Edinburgh University Press.

Todaeva, Bulyash (1961). *Dunsianskii iazyk* [The Dongxiang language]. Moskva: Izd-vo vostochnoi lit-ry.

Wan, Minggang 万明钢 (1991). Hàn, zàng, dōngxiāng zú 9-12 suì értóng hànyǔ bèidòng jù lǐjiě shuǐpíng de kuà wénhuà bǐjiào yánjiū 汉、藏、东乡族9-12岁儿童汉语被动句理解水平的跨文化比较研究 [A cross-cultural comparative study of the passive sentence comprehension level of 9-12-year-old children belonging to the Han, Tibetan and Dongxiang ethnic groups]. *Xinli Kexue*, (2), 61–69.

Wittmann, Henri, (1993). 'Relexification et créologenèse'. In André Crochetière, Jean-Claude Boulander and Conrad Quellon (eds), *Actes du XVe Congrès international des linguistes*, vol. 15, no. 4, pp. 335–338 Québec: Presses de l'Université Laval.

Wu, Hugjiltu (2003). 'Bonan'. In Janhunen, Juha (ed.), *The Mongolic Languages*, pp. 325–345. London, New York: Routledge Language Family.

Xi, Yuanlin 席元麟 (1995), 'Kāngjiā huízú huà de cíhuì tèdiǎn' 康家回族话的词汇特点 [Specificities of the Kangjia vocabulary spoken by the Hui]. *Qinghai Minzu Yanjiu*, 2, 52–58.

Xie, Xiaodong 谢小冬, Wang, Xunling 王勋陵, An, Li zhe 安黎哲, et al. (2002). 'Cóng qúntǐ yǐ zhuǎn de DNA xiànsuǒ kàn dōngxiāng zú de zú yuán wèntí' 从群体已转的DNA线索看东乡族的族源问题 [On the Origin of Dongxiang Nationality: Evidences from Community's DNA Evolution]. *Minzu yanjiu*, 1, 35–41.

Xu, Dan (2015a). 'Sinitic Languages of Northwest China: Where Did Their Case Marking Come From?'. In Cao, Guangshun 曹广顺, Redouane Djamouri, and Alain Peyraube (eds). *Languages in Contact in North China, Historical and Synchronic Studies*, vol. 13, pp. 217–244. Paris: Collection des cahiers de linguistique Asie Orientale.

Xu, Dan (2015b). 'Tangwang Initials'. In Cao, Guangshun 曹广顺, Redouane Djamouri, and Alain Peyraube (eds), *Languages in Contact in North China, Historical and Synchronic Studies*, vol. 13, pp. 319–338. Paris: Collection des cahiers de linguistique Asie Orientale.

Zhang, Lijie 张利洁, and Wang, Xilong 王希隆 (2006). 'Shānqū dōngxiāng zú xiǎoxuéshēng chuòxué wèntí de diàochá yǔ sīkǎo – yǐ dōngxiāngzú zìzhìxiàn běilǐngxiāng wéilì' 山区东乡族小学生辍学问题的调查与思考 – 以东乡族自治县北岭乡为例 [Investigation and reflection on the problem of dropouts among Dongxiang students in mountainous areas: a case study of Beiling Township, Dongxiang Autonomous County], *Minzu yanjiu* (2), 21–29, 107.

Zhao, Shiyu 赵世瑜 (2006). 'Zǔxiān jìyì, jiāyuán xiàngzhēng yǔ zúqún lìshǐ – shānxī hóng dòng dà huái shù chuánshuō jiěxī' 祖先记忆、家园象征与族群历史 – 山西洪洞大槐树传说解析[Ancestral memory, homeland symbol and ethnic history – an analysis of the legend of the Big Huai Tree in Hongdong, Shanxi], *Lishi Yanjiu*, 01, 49–64, 190–191.

Zhong, Jinzen 钟进文 (2007). *Gān qīng dìqū tèyǒu mínzú yǔyán wénhuà de qūyù tèzhēng* 甘青地区特有民族语言文化的区域特征 [Regional characteristics of the unique languages and cultures of the Gansu-Qinghai region]. Beijing: Zhongyang minzu daxue chubanshe.

Zhou, Minglang (2003). *Multilingualism in China: The Politics of Writing Reforms for Minority Languages, 1949–2002*. Walter de Gruyter.

Zuev, Yury (1960). 'Horse Tamgas from Vassal Princedoms (Translation of the Chinese Composition of VIII–X Centuries Tanhuyyao)', *Works of History, Archeology and Ethnography Institute*, VIII, 93–140.

Appendix

A.1 Questionnaire

The below questionnaire was initially prepared in Chinese, but the interviews were conducted in Dongxiang orally. Translations in English provided in brackets were not initially part of the questionnaire.

东乡语言状况调查

[A survey of the linguistic situation in Dongxiang]

此问表只做学术研究, 且不记您的姓名,因此不会对您产生任何影响! 请根据事实情况填写答案代号合作答,谢谢您的配合! [This questionnaire is for academic research purpose only. Your name will not be recorded, so it will not affect you in any way. Please fill in the answer code according to the facts, thank you for your cooperation!]

性别 : ___ 年龄 : ___ 职业 : ________
[Gender : ___ Age : ___ Occupation : ________]

(一) 您觉得自己主要是哪一个身份? ( ) [Which identity do you see yourself primarily as?]
□ 东乡族 [Dongxiang nationality] □ 回族 [Hui nationality]
□ 穆斯林人[Muslim] □ 中国人 [Chinese citizen]

您家有___ 口人 每人年龄为________________________

[There are ___ people in your family, each of whom is aged ______________]

其中几位会说汉语? ___位 [How many of them speak Chinese? ___]

(三) 受教育程度 ( ) [Level of education]

□ 文盲 [illiterate]
□ 小学 [elementary]
□ 初中[middle school]
□ 高中或专 [high school or college]
□ 大专以上 [post-secondary or above]

(四) 您主要通过哪种途程学习汉语拼音 (可多选) ( )
[Which is the main channel through which you learnt Hanyu Pinyin (Multiple answers allowed)]

□ 家庭 [Family]
□ 学校 [School]
□ 电视等媒体 [TV and other media]
□ 与会说汉语的居民日常接触 [Daily contact with Chinese-speaking residents]
□ 跟外面的人学 [Learning with people from the outside]
□ 其它 (请注明) [Others (please specify)]

(五) 您觉得您自己的汉语水平 ( ) [According to your own judgement, which answer best describes your knowledge of the Chinese language?]

□ 是完全不会 [don't know Chinese at all]
□ 会一点 [know a little]
□一般都可以交流 [can generally communicate]
□ 很好 [very good]

(六) 您觉得汉语是 ( ) [Do you think Chinese is]

□ 因为表示文化教育水平高而用 [used because it reveals a high level of culture and education]
□ 因为社会各个方面的需求要用 [used because of the needs of all aspects of society]
□ 因为社会各个方面的需求才要用 [used because of the needs of all aspects of society]
□ 没感觉 [I have no opinion]

(七) 您对东乡族人都成为“东乡语 汉语”双语人的态度是什么? ( )
[What's your opinion towards the fact that all Dongxiang people are bilingual in Dongxiang and Chinese?]
□ 迫切希望 [I hope they all become bilinguals]
□ 顺其自然 [I think it a natural process]
□ 无所谓 [I don't care]
□ 不希望 [I hope it does not happen]

(八) 您汉语 ( ) [Regarding speaking Chinese language]
□ 很喜欢用[I enjoyed using it]
□ 喜欢用 [I like using it]
□ 不太喜欢用 [I don't really like using it]
□ 不喜欢用 [I don't like using it]
□ 没感觉 [I have no opinion]

(九) 您为自己会说东乡语的东乡族的一员而自豪 ( )
You are proud to be a member of the Dongxiang ethnic group who speaks the Dongxiang language ( )
□ 非常自豪 [very proud]
□ 比较自豪 [pretty proud]
□ 不太自豪 [not too proud]
□ 没感觉 [I have no opinion]

(十) 您觉得东乡语是 ( ) [Do you think Dongxiang language is]
□ 一种传统语言, 一定要保护它 [a traditional language, it must be preserved.]
□ 东乡语不太重要, 不保护也没关系 [Dongxiang language is not very important, it doesn't matter if we don't preserve it.]
□ 东乡语是东乡社会发展的一个障碍 [Dongxiang language is an obstacle to the development of the Dongxiang society.]
□ 没感觉 [I have no opinion]

您是否支持孩子学习东乡语 ( )[Do you support your child to learn Dongxiang language]
□ 支持 [yes] □ 不支持 [no]

(十二) 您愿意把子女送到什么学校学习? ( ) [What kind of school would you like to send your child to?]

□ 用汉语授课的学校[Schools that teach only Chinese]

□ 用汉语和东乡语授课的学校 [Schools that teach in both Chinese and Dongxiang language]

(十三) 您平常在家庭说 ( ) At home, you usually speak

□ 东乡语 [Dongxiang language]

□ 汉语 [Chinese]

□ 两种语言都说 [both languages]

您平常在工作时说 ( ) [At work, you usually speak]

□ 东乡语 [Dongxiang language]

□ 汉语 [Chinese dialect]

□ 普通话 [Putonghua]

□ 以上都用 [I use all these languages]

如果有人在外地学习或工作几年后回到家乡, 不再说东乡语, 您如何看待? ( ) [How do you feel when someone who has studied or worked outside Dongxiang for a few years returns to Dongxiang and does not speaks the Dongxiang language?]

□ 可以理解 [It's understandable]

□ 反感 [I am opposed to it]

□ 听着别扭 [It sounds awkward]

□ 无所谓 [It doesn't matter]

如果您家里的孩子不会说东乡语, 您的态度是什么? ( )
[How would you feel if a child in your family does not speak the Dongxiang language?]

□ 同意 [I agree]

□ 无所谓 [It doesn't matter]

□ 反对 [I'm opposed to it]

A.2 Dongxiang Story

The following text is part of the corpus of spontaneous speech recorded during the field survey in 2009, which was subsequently transcribed and annotated.

"The white snake" (Chighan mogvei)
Recorded on 09/06/2009 in Suonanba

"The white snake" (*Chighan mogvei*)
Recorded on 2009/06/09 in Suonanba

(1) Hhe xienzi-de nie bieri gie-ne, ingiese gie-de nanxiong gie-ne.
DEM moment-LOC one spouse say-IPFV then house-LOC poor say-IPFV
'Once upon a time, a woman whose household was very poor'

(2) Ingiese nie fa-de ene jienqi echi-zho gie-ne.
then one time-LOC DEM menstruations go-PROG say-IPFV
'Once, she got her periods'

(3) Ingiese yama chinjiku wu gie-ne.
Then what thing POSS.NEG say-IPFV
'But she did not have anything to protect herself'

(4) Ingiese ne kun ghadun-ne gie echi-de shido gie-dene
Then DEM person father-in-law-R house go-SUC clean-SUC
yawu-ne.
go-IPFV
'Then, she went to her father-in-law to clean up his house'

(5) Ghadun-ni nie horase tasitari-ni wai-ne.
Father-in-law-3R one old turban-3R have-IPFV
'She found an old turban at her father-in-law that belonged to him'

(6) Ingiese, ghadun-ne tasitari bari-de chi-zhiwo gie-ne.
then father.in.law-R turban grap-SUC go-PROG say-IPFV
'So, she tool her father-in-law's turban and used it'

(7) Ingiese huaiyun gie, beye jiere olu-ne.
Then pregnant AUX body on get-IPFV
'Then she got pregnant, she got pregnant'

(8) Ingiese nie hon-de liangge.yue olu-zhi dou lie olu-na.
then one year-LOC two.month arrive-SIM all NEG give.birth-IPFV
'After a year and two months, she still did not give birth'

(9) Kieli-ni fugie fugie qiningie olu da-ne.
belly-R big big like.this give.birth cannot-IPFV
'Her belly was enormous, but she could not deliver'

(10) Ingiese kun-la-de asa-zho kun-la-de lie mejie-ne
then people-PL-LOC ask-PROG people-PL-LOC NEG know-IPFV

gie-zho.
say-PROG
'So they asked everybody, but nobody knew what was happening'

(11) Duwachi asa-zho, duwachi ulie mejie-ne.
sorcerer ask-PROG sorcerer NEG know-IPFV
'They asked the sorcere, but he did not know'

(12) Yiyen-de daifu-la pese ulie mejie-ne.
hospital-LOC doctor-PL again NEG know-IPFV
'The doctors at the hospital did not know either'

(13) Ingiese ene kun laoji-de-ne kielie-zho, nie kun
then DEM man spouseLOC-R talk-PROG DEM man

nie bowa asa echi-ne.
one imam ask go-IPFV
'So, someone said to the husban of that woman to go ask an Imam'

(14) Ingiese bowa kielie-zho :'ene yama-ni khuixin shi
then imam talk-PROG DEM what-GEN bad thing

gie-zho intu lie OLU-NA gie-zhi.
do-PROG like.this NEG give.birth-IPFV say SIM

'The Imam said: "this woman must have done something wrong, that is why she is not giving birth"'

(15) Ana-ni chi kielie-ni otu kie-se alama-de echi."
mom-3R 2 belly-ACC hurt go-CAUS cave-LOC go
'Talk to the mother and tell her that, when her belly will hurt, she must go to a cave'

(16) Nie olu-de khuina-ne bu uzhe-zhi.
one give.birth-SUC behind-R NEG look-SIM
'When she will have given birth, she will have to go without looking back'

(17) Kieli otu-zhi, giedon udu bai-se hhe bieri kieli otu gie-ne.
belly hurt-SIM few days be-SUC 3 spouse belly hurt say-IPFV
'Her belly started to hurt, a few days after, her belly started to hurt.'

(18) Ingiese alama-de echi gie-zhi, alama-de echi-se olu gie-ne.
then cave-LOC go say-SIM cave-LOC go-SUC give.birth say-IPFV
'Then she went to the cave, and gave birth there'

(19) Ingiese, bowa kielie-ku shi khuina-ne bu uzhe gie-zhuo.
then imam say-NOM COP behind-R NEG look say-PROG
'The Imam had said not to look back.'

(20) Ingiese olu-zhi ingie-dene khuina-ne echi-dene se uzhe-zhuo.
then give.birth-SIM then-SUC behind-R go-SUC NEG look-PROG
'Once she gave birth, the woman left without looking back'

(21) Ingie-dene banlu jiere echi-dene khuina uzhe gie-ne.
then-SUC half.way on go-SUC behind look say-IPFV
'But then, when she was half way (home), she looked back.'

(22) Yan gie-se gie-zhi !
What do-PST say-SIM
'What have she done!'

(23) Khuina-ne nie uzhe-se yane nie mogvei dagva ire-wo
behind-R one look-CAUS something one snake follow come-PFV

gie-ne.
say-IPFV
'She just took a look and saw that something like a snake was following her'

(24) Ingiese mogvei dagva-se ghujigvan-de yawu-zho gie-ne.
then snake follow-SUC quickly-MAN go-PROG say-IPFV
'Then the snake started to go faster and faster'

(25) Ingiese ne mogvei dagva gie-de ire-zho gie-ne.
then DEM snake follow house-LOC come-PROG say-IPFV
'The snake followed her home'

(26) Ingiese laoji-ni ire-se ene kun bieri-ni gogo-ni
then spouse-3R come-CAUS DEM man spouse-3R breast-3R
amala-zhi ire-zhuo gie-ne.
bite-SIM come-PROG say-IPFV
'Then, her husband came back and the snake came close to the woman's breast to suckle'

(27) Ingiese hhe bieri-ji ayi fugu-zho gie-zho.
then DEM woman-ACC scared die-PROG say-PROG
'And then this woman died of fright'

(28) Ingiese laoji-ni nie banda-sane usu sudoro gie-ne,
then spouse-3R one catch-IMM water inside do-IPFV

usu sudoro bundasa-ne.
water inside through-IPFV
'The husband caught the snake and through it immediately to the water'

(29) Hhe mogvei jiu bienji-dene chighan tastari gholo-ne gie-ne.
DEM snake so change-SUC white turban change-IPFV say-PROG
'The snake then changed into a white turban'

(30) Ingiese kun-la-ne man mejie gie-zhi ene shi yan gie-se
then people-PL-R all know say-SIM DEM COP what do-CAUS

nie gie-zhuo.
one say-PROG
'Then, everybody understood what happened'

(31) Pese bara !
again finish
'Finished!'

Index

ŁÓDŹ STUDIES IN LANGUAGE

Vol. 1 Barbara Lewandowska- Tomaszczyk / Patrick James Melia (eds): PALC'99: Practical Applications in Language Corpora. Papers from the International Conference at the University of Łódź, 15-18 April 1999. 2000.

Vol. 2 Lou Burnard / Tony McEnery (eds): Rethinking Language Pedagogy from a Corpus Perspective. Papers from the Third International Conference on Teaching and Language Corpora. 2000.

Vol. 3 Barbara Lewandowska-Tomaszczyk / John Osborne / Frits Schulte: Foreign Language Teaching and Information and Communication Technology. 2001.

Vol. 4 Piotr Cap: Explorations in Political Discourse. Methodological and Critical Perspectives. 2002.

Vol. 5 Ewa Waniek- Klimczak / Patrick James Melia (eds): Accents and Speech in Teaching English Phonetics and Phonology. EFL perspective. 2002.

Vol. 6 Barbara Lewandowska-Tomaszczyk / Kamila Turewicz (eds): Cognitive Linguistics Today. 2002.

Vol. 7 Barbara Lewandowska-Tomaszczyk (ed): PALC 2001: Practical Applications in Language Corpora. 2003.

Vol. 8 Corpus Linguistics by the Lune. A Festschrift for Geoffrey Leech. Edited by Andrew Wilson, Paul Rayson and Tony McEnery. 2003.

Vol. 9 Barbara Lewandowska-Tomaszczyk (ed): Practical Applications in Language and Computers. PALC 2003. 2004.

Vol. 10 Imagery in Language. Festschrift in Honour of Professor Ronald W. Langacker. Edited by Barbara Lewandowska-Tomaszczyk and Alina Kwiatkowska. 2004.

Vol. 11 Seana Coulson / Barbara Lewandowska-Tomaszczyk (eds): The Literal and Nonliteral in Language and Thought. 2005.

Vol. 12 Piotr Cap (ed): Pragmatics Today. 2005.

Vol. 13 Jacek Waliński / Krzysztof Kredens / Stanisław Goźdź-Roszkowski (eds): Corpora and ICT in Language Studies. PALC 2005. 2007.

Vol. 14 Krzysztof Kosecki (ed): Perspectives on Metonymy. Proceedings of the International Conference "Perspectives on Metonymy", held in Łódź, Poland, May 6-7, 2005. 2007.

Vol. 15 Barbara Lewandowska-Tomaszczyk / Tomasz Płudowski / Dolores Valencia Tanno (eds): The Media and International Communication. 2007.

Vol. 16 Krzysztof Kredens / Stanisław Goźdź-Roszkowski (eds): Language and the Law: International Outlooks. 2007.

Vol. 17 Barbara Lewandowska-Tomaszczyk (ed.): Corpus Linguistics, Computer Tools, and Applications – State of the Art. PALC 2007. 2008.

Vol. 18 Barbara Lewandowska-Tomaszczyk / Katarzyna Dziwirek (eds): Studies in Cognitive Corpus Linguistics. 2009.

Vol. 19 Barbara Lewandowska-Tomaszczyk / Marcel Thelen (eds): Meaning in Translation. 2010.

Vol. 20 Łukasz Bogucki / Krzysztof Kredens (eds): Perspectives on Audiovisual Translation. 2010.

Vol. 21 Piotr Stalmaszczyk (ed): Turning Points in the Philosophy of Language and Linguistics. 2011.

Vol. 22 Stanisław Goźdź-Roszkowski: Patterns of Linguistic Variation in American Legal English. A Corpus-Based Study. 2011.

Vol. 23 Kamila Ciepiela (ed): Identity through a Language Lens. 2011.

Vol. 24 Stanisław Goźdź-Roszkowski (ed): Explorations across Languages and Corpora. PALC 2009. 2011.

Vol. 25 Krzysztof Kosecki / Janusz Badio (eds): Cognitive Processes in Language. 2012.

Vol. 26 Alina Kwiatkowska (ed): Texts and Minds. Papers in Cognitive Poetics and Rhetoric. 2012.

Vol. 27 Paul A. Wilson (ed): Dynamicity in Emotion Concepts. 2012.

Vol. 28 Piotr Pęzik (ed): Corpus Data across Languages and Disciplines. 2012.

Vol. 29 Mikołaj Deckert: Meaning in Subtitling. Toward a Contrastive Cognitive Semantic Model. 2013.

Vol. 30 Łukasz Bogucki: Areas and Methods of Audiovisual Translation Research. 3rd Revised Edition. 2019.

Vol. 31 Janusz Badio / Kamila Ciepiela (eds): Language, Action, Interaction. 2013.

Vol. 32 Barbara Lewandowska-Tomaszczyk / Krzysztof Kosecki (eds): Time and Temporality in Language and Human Experience. 2014.

Vol. 33 Iwona Witczak-Plisiecka (ed): Cognitive and Pragmatic Aspects of Speech Actions. 2014.

Vol. 34 Małgorzata Anna Kamińska: A History of the Concise Oxford Dictionary. 2014.

Vol. 35 Łukasz Bogucki / Mikołaj Deckert (eds): Accessing Audiovisual Translation. 2015.

Vol. 36 Joanna Jabłońska-Hood: A Conceptual Blending Theory of Humour. Selected British Comedy Productions in Focus. 2015.

Vol. 37 Krzysztof Kosecki / Janusz Badio (eds): Empirical Methods in Language Studies. 2015.

Vol. 38 Katarzyna Stadnik: Chaucer's Choices. Through the looking-glass of medieval imagery. 2015.

Vol. 39 Paulina Pietrzak / Mikołaj Deckert (eds): Constructing Translation Competence. 2015.

Vol. 40 Małgorzata Fabiszak / Karolina Krawczak / Katarzyna Rokoszewska (eds): Categorization in Discourse and Grammar. 2016.

Vol. 41 Marcel Thelen / Gys-Walt van Egdom / Dirk Verbeeck / Łukasz Bogucki / Barbara Lewandowska-Tomaszczyk (eds): Translation and Meaning. New Series, Vol. 1. 2016.

Vol. 42 Łukasz Bogucki / Barbara Lewandowska-Tomaszczyk / Marcel Thelen (eds): Translation and Meaning. New Series, Vol. 2, Pt. 1. 2016.

Vol. 43 Łukasz Bogucki / Barbara Lewandowska-Tomaszczyk / Marcel Thelen (eds): Translation and Meaning. New Series, Vol. 2, Pt. 2. 2016.

Vol. 44 Przemysław Łozowski / Katarzyna Stadnik (eds): Visions and Revisions. Studies in Theoretical and Applied Linguistics. 2016.

Vol. 45 Marek Kuźniak / Bożena Rozwadowska / Michał Szawerna (eds): From Motion to Emotion. Aspects of Physical and Cultural Embodiment in Language. 2016.

Vol. 46 Anna Rędzioch-Korkuz: Opera Surtitling as a Special Case of Audiovisual Translation. Towards a Semiotic and Translation Based Framework for Opera Surtitling. 2016.

Vol. 47 Mateusz Sajna: Video Game Translation and Cognitive Semantics. 2016.

Vol. 48 Kamila Ciepiela (ed): Identity in Communicative Contexts. 2016.

Vol. 49 Mikołaj Nkollo: The Entrenchment of the 'unus alterum' Pattern. Four Essays on Latin and Old Romance Reciprocal Constructions. 2016.

Vol. 50 Paweł Rydzewski: Backness Distinction in Phonology. A Polish Perspective on the Phonemic Status of y. 2016.

Vol. 51 Piotr Pęzik / Jacek Tadeusz Waliński (eds): Language, Corpora and Cognition. 2017.

Vol. 52 Janusz Badio (ed): Events and Narratives in Language. 2016.

Vol. 53 Mikołaj Deckert (ed): Audiovisual Translation – Research and Use. 2017. 2nd Expanded Edition 2019.

Vol. 54 Michał Szawerna: Metaphoricity of Conventionalized Diegetic Images in Comics. A Study in Multimodal Cognitive Linguistics. 2017.

Vol. 55 Artur Gałkowski / Monika Kopytowska (eds): Current Perspectives in Semiotics. Signs, Signification, and Communication. 2018.

Vol. 56 Artur Gałkowski / Monika Kopytowska (eds): Current Perspectives in Semiotics. Text, Genres, and Representations. 2018.

Vol. 57 Łukasz Bogucki / Piotr Cap (eds): Exploration in Language and Linguistics. For Professor Piotr Stalmaszczyk on the Occasion of His 60th Birthday. 2018.

Vol. 58 Michał Kornacki: Computer-assisted Translation (CAT) Tools in the Translator Training Process. 2018.

Vol. 59 Marcin Walczyński / Piotr Czajka / Michał Szawerna (eds): On the Verge between Language and Translation. 2018.

Vol. 60 Łukasz Bogucki / Paulina Pietrzak / Michał Kornacki (eds): Understanding Translator Education. 2018.

Vol. 61 Marcin Walczyński: Psycho-Affective Factors in Consecutive Interpreting. 2019.

Vol. 62 Kamila Ciepiela (ed): Language, Identity and Community. 2019.

Vol. 63 Olga Łabendowicz: Audiovisual Translation in Poland. Changing Audiences. 2019.

Vol. 64 Enrique Bernárdez / Joanna Jabłońska-Hood / Katarzyna Stadnik (eds): Cognition in context. New insights into language, culture and the mind. 2019.

Vol. 65 Montse Corrius / Eva Espasa / Patrick Zabalbeascoa (eds): Translating Audiovisuals in a Kaleidoscope of Languages. 2019.

Vol. 66 Barbara Lewandowska-Tomaszczyk / Valeria Monello / Marco Venuti (eds): Language, Heart, and Mind. Studies at the intersection of emotion and cognition. 2020.

Vol. 67 Marta Chodkiewicz: Understanding the Development of Translation Competence. 2020.

Vol. 68 Urszula Paradowska: Developing Information Competence in Translator Training. 2021.

Vol. 69 Luca Valleriani: Upper-class English in Natural and Audiovisual Dialogue. 2021.

Vol. 70 Michał Kornacki and Gary Massey (eds): Contextuality in Translation and Interpreting. Selected Papers from the Łódź-ZHAW Duo Colloquium on Translation and Meaning 2020–2021. 2022.

Vol. 71 Monika Kopytowska / Artur Gałkowski / Massimo Leone (eds): Thought- Sign-Symbol. Cross-Cultural Representations of Religion. 2022.

Vol. 72 Bartosz Pietrzak: The Concept of Honor in the Language of Early Arabic Poetry. A Cultural Linguistic Study. 2022.

Vol. 73 Aleksandra Beata Makowska: Terminology and phraseology in research papers in the domains of new technologies. A cognitive corpus-based perspective. 2024.

Vol. 74 Marco Venuti / Emanuela Campisi / Ester Di Silvestro (eds): Strategies of Inclusion and Exclusion in online and offline Interaction. 2024.

Vol. 75 Łukasz Dutka: The Quality of Live Subtitling. Technology, User Expectations and Quality Metrics. 2024.

Vol. 76 Klaudia Gajewska: Voice Assistants in Action-oriented Mediation Practice. 2025.

Vol. 77 Julie Lefort: Overview of the Sociolinguistic Context of the Dongxiang Language. 2025.

www.peterlang.com

www.ingramcontent.com/pod-product-compliance
Ingram Content Group UK Ltd.
Pitfield, Milton Keynes, MK11 3LW, UK
UKHW041828100926
8556IPUK00002B/80

9 783631 921814